Nature's Changes

Metamorphosis

Changing Bodies

Bobbie Kalman

🌳 Crabtree Publishing Company

www.crabtreebooks.com

Created by Bobbie Kalman

Dedicated by Bryan Kivell
With love to Mom, Dad, Adam, and Lesley

Editor-in-Chief
Bobbie Kalman

Writing team
Bobbie Kalman
Kelley MacAulay
Kathryn Smithyman

Editors
Molly Aloian
Robin Johnson
Reagan Miller

Design
Margaret Amy Salter
Samantha Crabtree (cover)
Robert MacGregor (series logo)

Production coordinator
Katherine Berti

Photo research
Crystal Sikkens

Consultant
Patricia Loesche, Ph.D., Animal Behavior Program,
Department of Psychology, University of Washington

Illustrations
Barbara Bedell: pages 16, 17, 28, 29, 31
Antoinette "Cookie" Bortolon: page 15 (top)
Katherine Berti: page 24
Margaret Amy Salter: series logo illustrations, pages 9, 11,
      12, 14, 15 (bottom-left and right)
Bonna Rouse: pages 4, 18-19, 20, 21, 22, 23

Photographs
© Dwight Kuhn: pages 11, 13 (left), 25
Robert McCaw: page 23
Minden Pictures: Rene Krekels/Foto Natura: page 24
Photo Researchers Inc.: G. I. Bernard: page 22; Andy Harmer: page 27;
      Jim Zipp: pages 12, 13 (middle and right), 14
Visuals Unlimited: Bill Beatty: page 20; Patrice Ceisel: page 21;
      Gary Meszaros: page 26; Dick Poe: pages 8, 10 (top)
Other images by Brand X Pictures, Corel, Digital Stock,
      Digital Vision, and Otto Rogge Photography

Crabtree Publishing Company

www.crabtreebooks.com   1-800-387-7650

Copyright © **2005 CRABTREE PUBLISHING COMPANY**.
All rights reserved. No part of this publication may be reproduced,
stored in a retrieval system or be transmitted in any form or by any
means, electronic, mechanical, photocopying, recording, or
otherwise, without the prior written permission of Crabtree
Publishing Company. In Canada: We acknowledge the financial
support of the Government of Canada through the Canada Book
Fund for our publishing activities.

Printed in Canada/102014/TT20140818

Cataloging-in-Publication Data
Kalman, Bobbie.
   Metamorphosis : changing bodies / Bobbie Kalman.
      p. cm. -- (Nature's changes series)
   Includes index.
   ISBN-13: 978-0-7787-2273-1 (RLB)
   ISBN-10: 0-7787-2273-2 (RLB)
   ISBN-13: 978-0-7787-2307-3 (pbk.)
   ISBN-10: 0-7787-2307-0 (pbk.)
   1. Metamorphosis--Juvenile literature. I. Title.
   QL981.K35 2005
   571.8'76--dc22

                                           2005000491
                                           LC

Published in Canada
Crabtree Publishing
616 Welland Ave.
St. Catharines, Ontario
L2M 5V6

Published in the United States
Crabtree Publishing
PMB 59051
350 Fifth Avenue, 59th Floor
New York, New York 10118

Published in the United Kingdom
Crabtree Publishing
Maritime House
Basin Road North, Hove
BN41 1WR

Published in Australia
Crabtree Publishing
3 Charles Street
Coburg North
VIC, 3058

Contents

Big changes

Most animals begin their lives inside eggs. Many animals look like their parents when they **hatch**, or break out of their eggs. These animals do not change very much as they grow.

baby sea turtle

Sea turtles are animals that do not change very much as they grow.

adult sea turtle

What is metamorphosis?

Some animals look nothing like their parents when they hatch. As these animals grow into adults, their bodies go through many changes. These changes are called **metamorphosis**. Metamorphosis means changing **form**, or shape.

This caterpillar will go through metamorphosis. When it has finished metamorphosis, it will look like the beautiful butterfly on the right.

Two kinds of changes

There are two kinds of metamorphosis.
One kind is called **complete metamorphosis**.
Insects that go through complete metamorphosis
change completely. They have four stages
in their lives. The four stages are egg, **larva**,
pupa, and adult. Insects such as butterflies and
ladybugs go through complete metamorphosis.

butterfly

ladybug

Three stages

The other kind of metamorphosis is called **incomplete metamorphosis**. Animals that go through incomplete metamorphosis have only three stages in their lives. The three stages are egg, **nymph**, and adult. Dragonflies and grasshoppers are insects that go through incomplete metamorphosis.

This dragonfly is an adult.

Butterfly eggs

Butterflies go through complete
metamorphosis. A butterfly begins
its life as a tiny baby inside an egg.
The baby looks like a little worm.
In its egg, the baby has food to eat.
The food is called **yolk**.

A tiny baby insect is growing inside this butterfly egg.

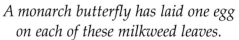

Eggs on plants

Different kinds of butterflies lay their eggs on different kinds of plants. For example, monarch butterfly mothers lay their eggs only on milkweed plants. If there are no milkweed plants, there will be no monarch butterflies!

A monarch butterfly has laid one egg on each of these milkweed leaves.

A larva grows quickly

After three to six days, the baby hatches from its egg. It chews its way out. It is now a larva. A butterfly larva is called a **caterpillar**. After hatching, the caterpillar eats its egg. The egg is full of **nutrients**. Nutrients help living things grow.

This monarch caterpillar is eating its egg.

Caterpillar bodies

There are many kinds of caterpillars. Not all caterpillars look the same. Some caterpillars are green, some are red, some are yellow, and some have stripes. Different kinds of caterpillars change into different kinds of butterflies.

Room to grow

A caterpillar is hungry! It has strong jaws for chewing leaves. It eats a lot and grows quickly, but its skin does not grow with its body. Eventually, its skin becomes too tight. The caterpillar must **molt**, or shed its skin. As it keeps eating, its body gets even bigger. The caterpillar grows and molts several times.

This monarch caterpillar has just finished molting. Its old skin is behind its body. The caterpillar eats its old skin because the skin contains many nutrients. Not all caterpillars eat their old skin.

Becoming a pupa

After many molts, a caterpillar gets ready for the next stage in its metamorphosis. It makes a strong string called **silk** inside its body. The caterpillar uses the silk string to attach itself to the branch of a tree. It then hangs upside down from the branch and molts one last time.

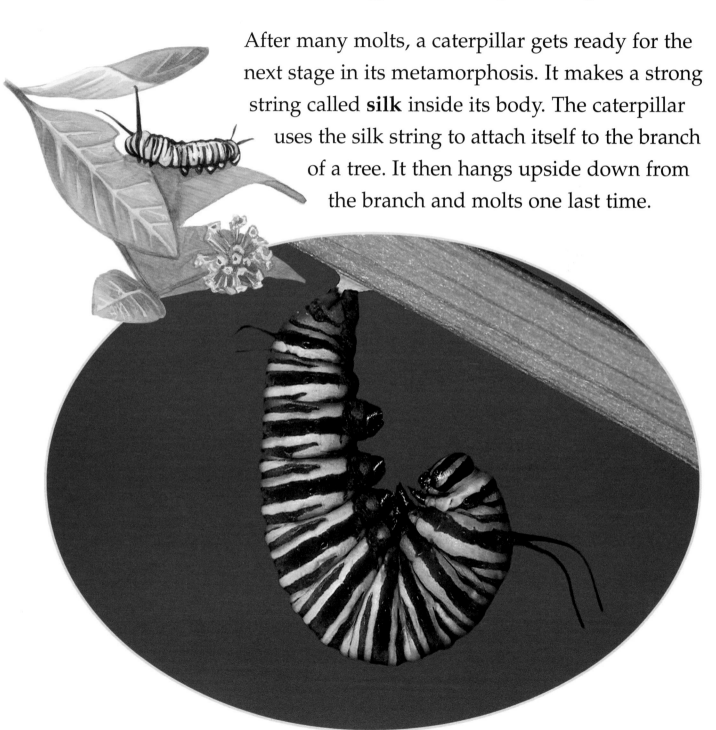

Inside the chrysalis

After the last molt, a hard case forms around the caterpillar's body. The case is called a **chrysalis**. Inside the chrysalis, the caterpillar's body changes completely. It turns into liquid. The insect is now a pupa. Little by little, the pupa grows body parts such as wings. It is changing into an adult butterfly.

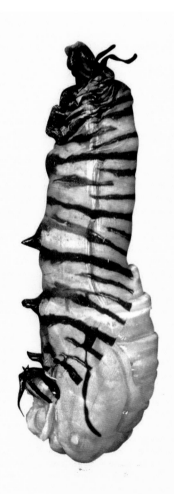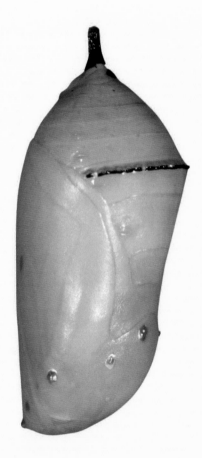

A chrysalis starts to form around the caterpillar's body.

Inside the chrysalis, the caterpillar's body is liquid.

When the chrysalis turns clear, the caterpillar has finished its metamorphosis. The adult butterfly is ready to break out of the chrysalis.

An adult butterfly

When the butterfly is fully formed, it pushes itself out of the chrysalis. It cannot fly yet because its wings are wet and weak. The butterfly hangs upside down from the chrysalis until its wings are dry and strong. The adult butterfly then flies away.

A new body

The caterpillar has now finished metamorphosis. It has changed into a butterfly. Look at the pictures below to see how the caterpillar's body has changed.

proboscis

The caterpillar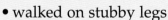

- walked on stubby legs
- did not have wings
- had strong jaws for chewing leaves
- had a long, thin yellow body with black and white stripes

The butterfly

- has six thin legs
- has two pairs of wings
- has a **proboscis** for sucking a sweet liquid called **nectar** from flowers
- has orange wings with black lines and white spots

Ladybug changes

A ladybug is a kind of beetle. It is another insect that goes through complete metamorphosis. Keep reading to learn how a ladybug's body changes as it goes through complete metamorphosis.

Inside the egg

Mother ladybugs lay groups of eggs. The baby ladybugs inside the eggs are in their first stage of metamorphosis. Each baby eats the yolk inside its egg and grows.

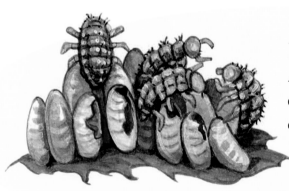

Life as a larva

A tiny larva hatches from each egg. Each larva goes off on its own to find food. A ladybug larva eats **aphids**. Aphids are tiny insects. As the larva grows, it molts four times.

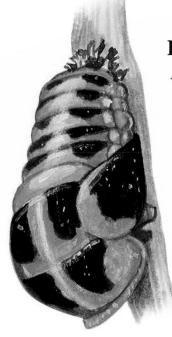

Pupa in a chrysalis

After its last molt, the larva attaches itself to a plant's leaf or stem. It makes a chrysalis around its body. Inside the chrysalis, the larva's body turns into liquid. The insect is now a pupa. Its adult body parts start to grow. When the pupa has all its adult parts, it breaks open its chrysalis.

Fly away, ladybug!

The adult ladybug pushes itself out of the chrysalis. It now has wings and can fly. The ladybug eats aphids, just as it did when it was a larva.

Frog changes

Frogs go through complete metamorphosis. The changes in the bodies of frogs are very different from the changes in the bodies of insects.

eggs

tadpoles

From egg to frog

Frogs begin their lives inside eggs. When they hatch, they are not frogs, however. They are **tadpoles**. As tadpoles go through metamorphosis, they become frogs. Some frogs go through metamorphosis in a few weeks. Others can take several months to finish metamorphosis.

frog

This tadpole will soon be a frog.

tadpoles

Eggs called spawn

Frogs lay their eggs in calm, shallow water. The eggs stick together in clumps. Clumps of frog eggs are called **spawn**. There can be thousands of eggs in a clump of spawn. The eggs look like balls of clear jelly. The jelly helps protect the tiny babies growing in the eggs. Some of the babies will become tadpoles.

Most of the eggs laid by a mother frog will never hatch. They will be eaten by turtles, fish, and other animals.

20

Time to hatch!

After about a week, a tadpole hatches from each egg. A tadpole has a head and a tail. It breathes through body parts called **gills**, just as fish do. At first, the tadpole cannot swim well. It rests on weeds or on other plants. As the tadpole grows stronger, it begins to swim around looking for tiny plants to eat.

A tadpole swims by moving its tail from side to side.

More tadpole changes

After the tadpole starts swimming, its body begins to change. The tadpole grows legs on both sides of its tail. As its back legs grow, its tail starts to shrink. Skin begins to cover its gills, and **lungs** form inside its body. Lungs are body parts that take in air and let out air. Soon, the tadpole grows front legs.

A tadpole uses its tiny teeth to eat insects and plants.

Becoming a frog

tadpole with a small tail

When its tail is almost gone, the tadpole looks more like a frog. It lives at the edge of a pond. It sometimes uses its new legs to crawl out of the water to look for insects to eat. The tadpole uses its lungs to breathe air. When its tail is completely gone, the tadpole has become an adult frog.

adult frog

A frog has strong legs for jumping and a long, sticky tongue for catching insects.

Dragonfly metamorphosis

Dragonflies are insects that go through incomplete metamorphosis. Dragonfly mothers lay their eggs in water or on plants near water. Some kinds of dragonfly babies grow inside their eggs for a few weeks. Other kinds of dragonfly babies grow inside their eggs for a few months.

A dragonfly mother lays her eggs in water. She lays many eggs at a time.

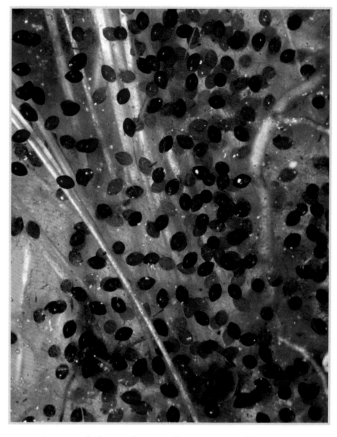

Some of these dragonfly eggs will be eaten by other animals, but many will survive.

Living under water

A nymph hatches from each egg.
It lives under water. It paddles
its six legs to swim. The nymph
breathes using gills. It has a
mouthpart called a **mask**.
The nymph stretches out its
mask to grab food. It eats tiny
insects, fish, and tadpoles.
The nymph in this picture
is eating a tadpole.

Eating and growing

A nymph eats a lot of food and grows quickly. As the nymph grows, lungs form inside its body. The nymph now needs to breathe air above water. It moves near the top of the water, where it can stick its head up to get breaths of air.

Many molts

As the nymph grows, its skin becomes too tight. The insect molts many times. After its first molt, the nymph begins to grow tiny wings. Each time the nymph molts, its wings grow a little bigger.

Tiny wings are starting to form on this dragonfly nymph's back.

Ready to fly!

Just before the nymph becomes an adult, it crawls out of the water and climbs onto a plant. On the plant, the nymph molts for the last time. It is now an adult dragonfly. Its wings are soft and wet. They are folded up. The dragonfly sits on the plant and unfolds its wings. When its wings become hard and dry, the dragonfly is ready to fly.

This nymph is molting for the last time. It is crawling out of its old skin. Its wings are wet.

The adult dragonfly is leaving its old skin behind. Its wings are unfolded and dry.

Grasshopper changes

A grasshopper is another insect that goes through incomplete metamorphosis. When a baby grasshopper hatches from its egg, it is a nymph. As the nymph grows, it changes into an adult grasshopper.

Eggs in soil

A mother grasshopper lays her eggs in soil. She covers the eggs with a white liquid that she makes inside her body. The liquid gets hard when it dries. It keeps the eggs warm. A baby grasshopper grows inside each egg.

These grasshopper eggs are safe and warm in the soil.

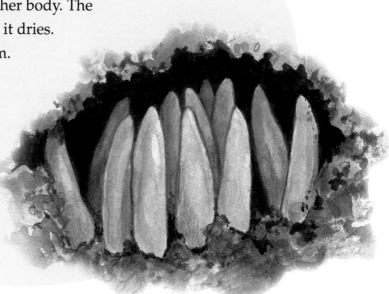

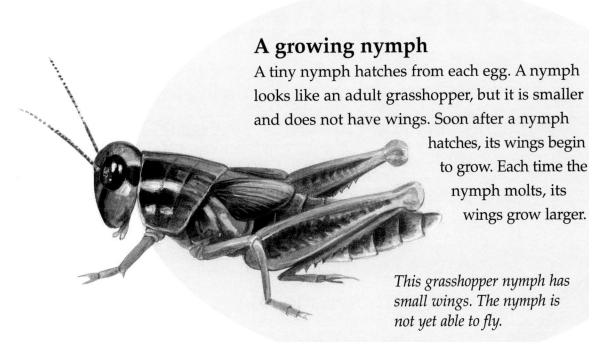

A growing nymph

A tiny nymph hatches from each egg. A nymph looks like an adult grasshopper, but it is smaller and does not have wings. Soon after a nymph hatches, its wings begin to grow. Each time the nymph molts, its wings grow larger.

This grasshopper nymph has small wings. The nymph is not yet able to fly.

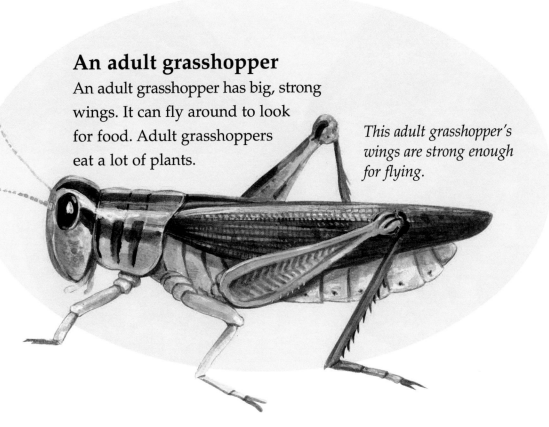

An adult grasshopper

An adult grasshopper has big, strong wings. It can fly around to look for food. Adult grasshoppers eat a lot of plants.

This adult grasshopper's wings are strong enough for flying.

Watch it change!

You have learned that metamorphosis means "a change of form." You can see animals change right before your eyes by making moving pictures. Read the instructions on the next page to learn how to make your own moving metamorphosis picture!

Choose an animal

Before you begin, look at the pictures in this book again. Choose an animal for your moving picture. You will need to draw two pictures of the same animal. One picture should show the animal before it has finished metamorphosis. The other should show an adult animal that has completed its metamorphosis.

Making moving pictures

1. First, cut two small squares out of a piece of paper.

2. Use pencil crayons to draw the two pictures. Draw one picture on one square and the other picture on the other square.

3. Once you have finished your drawings, tape your pictures back to back on the end of a straw or a pencil.

4. Hold the straw or pencil between your hands. To see your animal change shape, quickly rub your hands together to make the pictures spin.

Words to know

Note: Boldfaced words that are defined in the text may not appear in the glossary.

chrysalis A hard covering that forms around the body of an insect during the third stage of complete metamorphosis

gill A body part that takes oxygen from water

larva An insect that is in the second stage of complete metamorphosis

molt To shed a layer of skin

nutrient A substance that helps living things grow and stay healthy

nymph An insect that is in the second stage of incomplete metamorphosis

pupa An insect that is inside a chrysalis during the third stage of complete metamorphosis

spawn A mass of fish or frog eggs

Index

Made in the USA
Charleston, SC
19 April 2013

About } the author

Karen A. Chase is a writer, designer, photographer, and traveler. Born in Canada, she has lived in the United States since 1990. As a professional graphic designer and copywriter, she opened her own branding and design studio in 2004. A division of that studio is dedicated to creating book covers, trailers, and other materials solely for authors and publishers. While building her company, she branched into a secondary career as a freelance writer of historical fiction, poetry, and nonfiction, writing for online magazines like *HOW Design* and as a guest columnist for the *Richmond Times-Dispatch* newspaper. *Bonjour 40* is her first book. She and her partner, Ted, live in Richmond, Virginia with their two cats.

KarenAChase.com
224Pages.com & 224design.com

Julia –
Happy travel
planning.

Karen Chase

KAREN A. CHASE

a memoir by

A Paris Travel Log:
(40 years. 40 days. 40 seconds.)

BONJOUR 40

Cover & Book Design by 224pages.com

For more information about the author visit:
KarenAChase.com

ISBN 978-0-615-73814-7

To my travel bugs:

Mom and Dad for paving the runway.
Bruce and Telva for fueling the desire to take off.
Ted for making limitless the skies.

The real voyage of discovery
consists not in seeking new landscapes
but in having new eyes.

—*Marcel Proust*

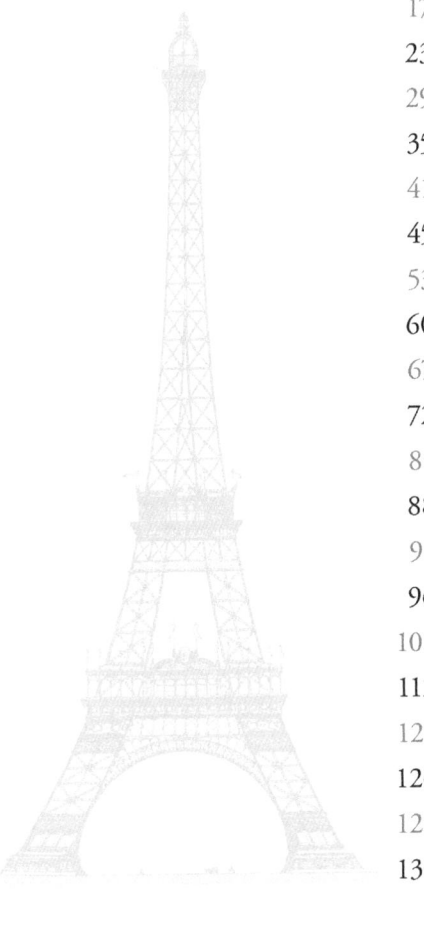

In my favorite city not long after I arrived. Hat. Heels. Purse with scarf. Bike in the background. In front of the tower. Trying to fit in, and feeling at home at the same time.

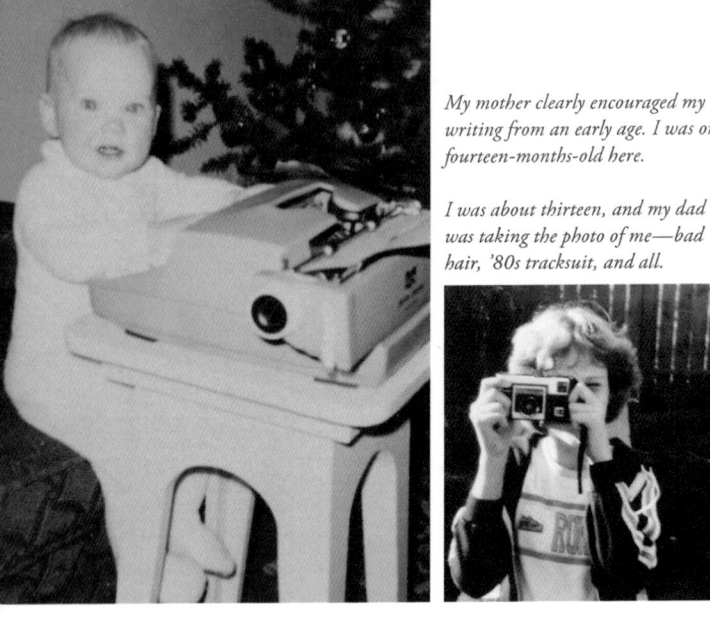

My mother clearly encouraged my writing from an early age. I was only fourteen-months-old here.

I was about thirteen, and my dad was taking the photo of me—bad hair, '80s tracksuit, and all.

{ *...giving that little girl in me the gift...* }

Beginning } Day 1 ~ March 4

Last year, I was asked if I was going to do anything special when I turned forty. Barely a day into my thirty-ninth birthday, and forty comes up? What?! Many women dread this, I know. I'm not the type to be in denial or in the fetal position over it, but if I absolutely had to turn forty, then I needed to figure out how best to do it. Or, better yet, where. So for the last year I've planned and saved, and in less than two months I will leave to celebrate for the whole month of May in Paris. The city of writers, light, and love. I'll live there for almost forty days—something I've wanted to do since I was a little girl.

Today marks my actual fortieth birthday. But quite frankly forty feels a lot like thirty-nine, which honestly felt a lot like twenty-nine except I have more money and more experience, and I'm certainly making better choices. Even though my age is 4-0, I can sincerely say there is a spirit in me that is still thirty, or twenty, or even ten. Perhaps it's because I'm giving that little girl in me the gift she's always wanted—a grand adventure. So to this birthday I say, Bonjour 40! I'm here. Let's begin…

Introduction }AUTHOR NOTES

This forty-day travel journal from my month-long trip to Paris began as a blog. Upon hearing about my impending trip, friends and family quickly said, "Be sure to send emails or pictures, or schedule some time to chat while you're there." How could I tell them no? I didn't want to be on the computer when I could be exploring Paris. I wanted to write a novel I'd been developing and disconnect for a while. To experience living *there*. Not to stay online with *here*. Finally a friend suggested producing a blog. "You could tell us about what you're doing, and you could include your photos because they're always so good." Brilliant. Another friend and neighbor suggested calling it, *Bonjour 40*.

Introduction } ...continued

So beginning on my birthday and for a total of forty days, I posted a photograph from my journey, along with a thought or two you could read in about forty seconds (give or take a few). Hence, forty years, forty days, forty seconds. I limited the length of the daily entries to prevent myself from rambling on, so I could get off my blasted computer and back to exploring and writing in Paris. My blog entries have become this book, slightly updated to feel less like an online blog and more like a journal. The photos from the original blog, where appropriate, are included in the book.

There were events, thoughts, or experiences along the way I wanted to share that were simply too involved for my forty-second format. So upon returning home, I sat in cafés with my same notebook (paper, not computer) and wrote the "reflection" pieces. They are written with the cumulative knowledge of my month-long stay, and through eyes that have completed the trip, but they are interspersed among the journal entries where they can provide deeper detail.

Many people have asked me how I managed to arrange the time and funds for this trip. I have a business to maintain and design clients with commitments, I'm in a happy relationship, and I am most certainly not a wealthy woman. I did not ask Ted nor my parents to help pay for this. I'm forty for heaven's sake, not eighteen and asking to backpack through Europe. For years, I thought this was one heck of an indulgent luxury few people could afford. Turns out it wasn't, and I could.

I could, because of long-term life choices about family (I am happily childless by choice), how I lived (not beyond my means), and how I built my career (into a solo design business). When I turned thirty-nine, I really put the live-in-Paris-for-a-month plan into action. I told everyone about my dream trip, so all my clients knew I would be gone. They were gracious enough to end and begin projects on either side of the trip. I saved money by asking myself, "Do I need to buy this dress, or is this dress a day in Paris?"

Friends who knew Paris helped me figure out where to live well, and within my budget. I opted not to contribute to my IRA for the year, and instead contributed to my L-I-F-E. I am forty. I have plenty of time to save for my old age.

I could also arrange to go on such an adventure because of Ted. He is my love and partner—an intelligent, funny, and affectionate Italian from New Jersey. He is referenced in many of the entries and joined me on day thirty. A psychotherapist, he fully believes in realizing dreams and said, "Go, and I will meet you. Find a tree for us to nap under, and tell me in which café we will meet when I arrive." He was excited for me right from the beginning. For that, I am so grateful. We agreed he would come near the end to ensure I would get on the plane and return home.

Kristen Weber, my editor, traveled with me through reading my blog, gave me great advice to ensure it was personal and not a travel guide, and helped me organize the additional entries into a readable, linear work. The only thing better than Kristen's insightful pen is the kindness evident in her comments. April Michelle Davis of Editorial Inspirations made sure my phrases, spelling, and tenses ~~were right. are correct.~~ were correct. All writers need editors as enthusiastic about our work as these two, so that throughout the critiques, our writing grows stronger, and we want to return to the words. *Merci beaucoup* to Mark Rankin and Jacquie Wiesner for reviewing the French.

Many of the restaurants or shops included are named as is, in the hope that others will follow the trail and find the apartment where I stayed, the café where Ted and I met upon his arrival, or the place where I drank the best *café crème*. During my time in Paris, I met many delightful people, but I've changed most of their names to give them a little privacy. They know who they are. A few agreed to be included, like my fellow writer and friend, Andrew Eddy, his family, and Dorothée who owned the crab shack at the end of my block. The other identity that had to remain the same is that of Dorothée's little Terrier, Bandit. There is just no better name for a patch-eyed dog that is constantly trying to steal food despite the fact that he works in a restaurant.

The ebook came out very soon after my trip, and since then, readers have visited with me through the words. A few of them have even been to Paris, my book in hand, and visited Dorothée and Bandit (who has adored the fame). This tangible, tactile book is for all those who begged for a print version, and for those who would prefer to hold Paris in their hands.

So come along, and let us travel to Paris together.

On Paris } Day 2 ~ March 25

On Paris, there simply are not enough guidebooks, maps, language lessons, recipes, stories, or tips for me. My friends, neighbors, and the bookstore gave me a steady supply of what-tos, what-not-tos, and how-tos to prepare for this trip. Somewhere in my fairy-tale head, I believe if I do enough reading and preparation I will step off the plane at the Charles De Gaulle airport and instantly be more French than the third-generation Mademoiselle kneading dough at the corner *Patisserie*. My romantic side would love to just spontaneously show up and wing it—wouldn't that after all be more French to live in the moment? I just can't do it. All my research is not merely because I'm a planning junkie with a Dutch-sensibility for list making. Invariably it's my curiosity that gets the better of me, and I simply have to know more. I want to be there before I arrive. I want to feel it on my skin like goose bumps that come up before you step from the warmth of the shower. I want my mouth to water merely from smelling it—like with warm, gooey brownies. I want the adventure to affect me before it's begun, so an information sponge I will be. So turn on the soundtrack from *French Kiss*, hand me *A Year in Provence* and a glass of wine, and let me get back to feeling like I'm already there.

My preparations for the trip included one-on-one tutoring, Fluenz DVDs, vicarious map exploration, advice from friends, and reading a variety of travel essays.

Packing } Day 3 ~ April 23

It always amazes me when packing for a trip how much stuff we can so quickly do without. I have seven bottles of goo, gel, lotions, and conditioners in my shower, but for a trip I only need one or two. I can wear the same three pairs of pants in Paris for a month, but not while I'm at home. I wouldn't consider myself a clothes junkie or a drug store diva, but in piling up and editing down what I'm taking on this trip I realize the importance of packing lightly. Certainly I'm taking a few solid pieces, so despite what the weather dishes out, I'll be able to keep on keeping on. And because it's Paris, I'm also taking a few pieces that are downright impractical. Then I can wear something whimsical in a land where no one knows me and I can feel like Carrie Bradshaw for fifteen minutes. But I also mean I'm packing lightly metaphorically. By leaving the clutter, the papers, the excess, the consuming world of things behind, I can get lost in the adventure, and not worry about keeping up with a bunch of stuff. So while I'm packing some necessary items—comfy clothes and shoes, a hat, sunscreen, a good book or two on my Kindle, and writing supplies—my focus is on the going, and not on the taking.

Panic } Day 4 ~ April 24

What, me worry? Yes. This feeling always happens to me the day before a trip. I throw three things in my bag I didn't want or need yesterday. I look at my airline ticket eighteen times. I set three alarm clocks and trust none of them. I review all of my lists. Did I get everything done? Did I pay that bill? Will I be okay? This is a five-week trip! I knew several weeks ago this feeling would come. Angst. I wouldn't be human if I wasn't filled with a little doubt or trepidation now and then, right? I mentioned it to a girlfriend at lunch one day, and in her very New York way she waved a hand at me and said, "Phfft, you'll be fine. Whatever." Thankfully a few things are in place to help me relax. Today I'm having breakfast with wonderful friends as if tomorrow is just another Monday. My flight is in the afternoon, so I can sleep well tonight. I also have a little image on my computer that has been helping me to relax. Last month I was in a library doing research for my novel, and I found a chair at an empty table. In front of me was a drawer, and just before I left, I opened it to see what was in there. Someone had carefully placed a hand-written sticky-note in the otherwise empty drawer. I smiled, took a picture, left it for the next curious reader who will pick that seat, and closed the drawer. It simply said, "Everything will be ok." Now that's a good sign.

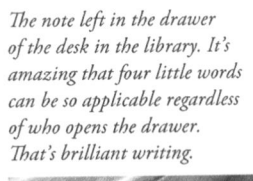

Even during my planning there was someone else who didn't want me to leave. Our cat Linus.

The note left in the drawer of the desk in the library. It's amazing that four little words can be so applicable regardless of who opens the drawer. That's brilliant writing.

{ *...I will miss our moments together...* }

Going } Day 5 ~ April 25

"I think I'm beginning to miss you already," Ted, my partner, said to me as we cuddled in a chair two weeks ago. Since then, his one little statement has given me a third eye to appreciate what is here, so I'll be sure to return. (Several friends think I won't come home, but I'll show them.) Ted's statement wasn't sadness or guilt. It was loving. I've been in relationships where I felt relieved to be away and alone, and quite simply that sucks. So now, I kind of cherish that little clenching feeling that says I will miss our moments together. Like reading together over breakfast. Or seeing those two dents in the bedroom pillows that remain after we get up—a reminder that even subconsciously we were together. That being said, I've traveled by myself before, so has he, so we each understand the importance of giving the gift of time alone. We've been planning what we'll do when he joins me a little over three weeks from now, but in the meantime, we both have things to do, and to miss. So on departure day this quote from *Out of Africa* seems fitting: "I am better at hello. It's an odd feeling… farewell. There is some envy in it… If we're tested at all, it's for patience… for doing without…" I think that's true both for those of us going, and those not quite yet.

Reflections } THE TRAVEL BUG

I caught the *travel bug* early. My family aptly named the desire to hit the road the travel bug because it indeed seemed like something contagious. I think there are a few ways to contract it. If you travel with someone already infected with wanderlust, they are sure to give you the bug because travelers can't stop talking about how wonderful it is. They'll breathe it all over you. Or you could pick it up in a foreign place because your system goes into culture shock and then adjusts, and you're never the same. Or you could even get it through osmosis by reading a book like *A Year in Provence* or *Murder on the Orient Express*. It's a sure thing you will come down with it if you combine all three.

The Travel Bug } ...continued

I got the bug from my parents who began by taking my older brother and me camping when I was a toddler, and then we all reinfected one another for the next fifteen years or so. My father was a teacher with no classes in July or August. He worked night classes during the year and my mother stretched every dollar he brought home so we could travel every summer, sometimes for six to ten weeks at a time. The four of us piled into cars, station wagons, pop-up and hard-wall trailers, and motor homes and made our way across forty states and nine Canadian provinces, through countless museums, on manufacturing tours, in and out of state parks, and buying new reading material in every used bookstore coast to coast. We had the bug. Bad.

Since then, I feel like I've spent the last twenty-five years building a life in between vacations and holidays. Don't get me wrong, I do find comfort with consistent routines. I've enjoyed my career as a designer and my new venture as a writer. Having a loving relationship nestled in our own home brings about a sense of balance and peace for me in many ways. But home to me also means "home base"—something I come back to when I need to or want to. Need to, because either the budget or the vacation days are limited. Or want to, for the familiarity and peace of a routine. Invariably though, within minutes of returning my head starts thinking about where to next. Not hours, not days. Minutes. Sometimes, and it's getting more and more this way, it's on the plane home or before the vacation is even over that it starts: "Where next? And when?"

Over the years, through Mexico, Canada, Europe, and more of the United States, I've planned trips. Like most, I've often packed as many places or events as I could into a couple of weeks. But I have also taken "move there" vacations. I moved from Calgary to San Antonio for school. To Roanoke, Virginia, for work. To Dallas to get divorced. Back to Virginia to find love again, and most recently to Richmond to build a life with Ted. What moving has given me is a sense of long-term vacation during times I couldn't afford to travel as much.

By living in a place for more than a few days or a week, I have been able to delve deeply into discovery. I have explored streets and shops the locals know exist, like Grandin Road and Too Many Books in Roanoke. I have discovered where, in San Antonio, to buy the most delicious tamales-to-go. They are at a small stand called Delicious Tamales-To-Go, I kid you not. I've been able to get to know the people and their customs and, better yet, see which habits to adopt that could improve my daily living regardless of my location.

When you get both the moving bug and the travel bug, it takes every ounce of your resolve to make a more permanent commitment, like owning a home or getting a dog. Cats, in my experience, tend to adapt. A sweet, small rescue cat named Colada lived with me until she was almost twenty, and together we moved through eighteen homes. Ted even joked about our nomad life, "Imagine how old she would have been if she had never moved." In addition to her, it does take an adventurous and confident partner like Ted to help create the balance of staying and going. He likes to travel, too, but has a business that requires consistency. Together, we've found a way to own a home, run our own businesses, and still be on the go.

All my experiences with moving and traveling made me think long and hard about the question my father posed to me on my thirty-ninth birthday: "Where are you going for your fortieth?" (Note: He did not ask what I wanted or what I was going to eat, but *where* I was going. That's the travel bug talking.)

I first came to Paris fifteen years ago, and from the moment I set foot in that city, I longed to move there. I can't afford to live in Paris full time. I can't get a visa, nor can I make a living as a designer because of the language issue. So, I thought, the next best thing is a short-term rental, and for this birthday *that* is something I could actually manage to do. *That* I could save for. *That* my life could work around. *That* I could share with Ted, or at least part of it. So once my dad asked the question, Paris very quickly seemed to be the right answer.

The best part was getting to feel more Parisian by the end of those five weeks. Was I? Heck no. Any Parisian, including the bum featured on Day 26 of this travel log will help explain why I am not. However, because I stayed for so long, I became a part of Paris, and it became a part of me. I can feel it. In my bones. In my heart.

I've been home a week now. On the plane back, I caught a terrible cold that turned into bronchitis. As I write this, I'm at the doctor's office (see last point above). I'm laughing to myself thinking I've really done it this time. I have such a bad case of moving + travel bug blues, that I might require medication. And yet even while sitting here on the examination table, I'm already wondering about where we should go for Ted's birthday next year. Sicily? Morocco? A sailboat in the Mediterranean? All three? And my parents celebrate their fiftieth next year, so that might be a trip home to Canada. But some of my girlfriends want to go somewhere… And… I hope the doctor has free samples because it's time to start saving my money again and working for where-next already.

Within the forty days of the trip, I came to further understand why move-there vacations are intoxicating: food, people, weather, places, everything is new. Along the way, I learned a lot, too. About traveling. About life. About others. About myself. A few of them include:

- Naps on the grass are essential to well-being.
- Walk more. Bike more.
- Learn new languages.
- Dress up a bit, even when alone. Why look shabby?
- Buy fresh flowers now and then.
- A scarf improves an outfit—for men and women.
- Fresh food is better than packaged food. Always.
- Be more polite.
- Laugh like the English.
- Kiss like the French.
- Always carry wet-wipes.
- Sharing a scene is better than stealing it.
- I can write anywhere.

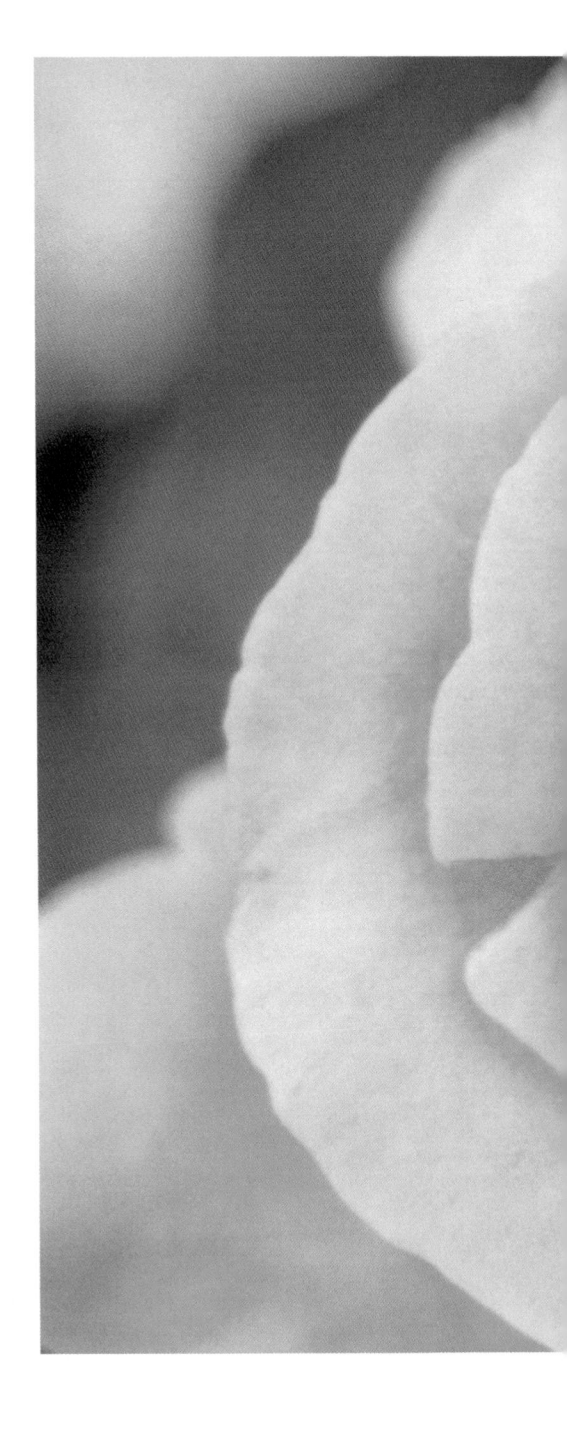

Paris is teeming with flower shops and roses.
This lovely blossom was found near Notre Dame.
Embrace the bloom and you embrace being Parisian.

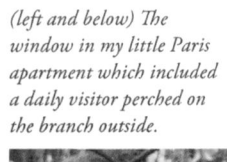

(far left) The view as I ate my first lunch.

(left and below) The window in my little Paris apartment which included a daily visitor perched on the branch outside.

Arriving } Day 6 ~ April 26

Je suis arrivée à Paris. A fairly uneventful flight landed me here at about 10 a.m. Paris time. Aside from a little settling in and unpacking, I simply walked around my neighborhood. Paris is set up in clockwise, circling, numbered districts called arrondissements—my rental apartment is near the Bastille and the Marais in the fourth arrondissement. Walking the 4e is a commitment of about seven hours to see about 1/10 of it. But (for the butt) that's a good thing after sitting on a plane for more than nine hours. As I wandered close to my new home, I made a few first-day observations:

~ Guys (and gals) on motorcycles here make motorcyclists in the United States look like six-year-olds on their first tricycles. Here, they fly at twice the speed of cars between the lanes of moving vehicles. As my taxi barreled along the Périphérique highway, I watched them fly between us and the cars in the next lane. At the exact moment I wondered if they were disobeying the law, I saw a motorcycle-cop doing 60 mph whip up the solid line between a Peugeot and a Mercedes.

~ Despite my jetlag and lack of sleep, it seems impossible to take a bad photograph. It will make editing my pictures even more difficult than I had imagined.

~ I'd like to blame my jetlag/lack of sleep on the undeniable fact that despite tutoring, CDs, books, and podcasts, my French quite frankly sucks. It's not the fault of the lessons, I'm sure. When I say, "Bonjour!" to anyone, the French coming at me seems faster than the motorcycles, and I can't keep up.

~ For a big city, the air is lovely here. Fresh, with the smells of baked goods and savory foods everywhere. It's 72º, sunny. A little cooler in the shade. Spring is blooming everywhere.

~ Through pointing at the lunch menu, what I inadvertently ordered today was flat-out amazing. Baked, buttered trout with almonds, ratatouille, and a café crème that made me cry.

After a shower and a cup of tea, I will take one last look out my lovely, treetop windows as the sun fades. I have managed to stay awake until about 9 p.m. and now the day must close. Paris will come in clearer tomorrow.

Women } Day 7 ~ April 27

Every American woman should visit Paris. I asked a waiter how to say, "I am full" in French. Word for word it would be, "*Je suis pleine*," however to say that in French means you're pregnant, so I knew that wasn't it. The waiter's response, however, perfectly summed up French women. "There is no translation. It would not be elegant for a woman to say that." And elegant they are, regardless of age or attire. The older women often have long hair, their expressions exude *individualité*, and they are proof if you constantly walk through the world very, very quickly in a pair of heels or ballet flats, your legs and figure will be just as remarkable at eighty as they were at twenty. I do believe part of their beauty and confidence must be this: No matter how challenging, how grim, or how lovely their individual lives may have been to this point, deep inside they know "at least I lived it in Paris." For this city, like her women, has such great character. Having just turned forty, I am thrilled to be seeing examples of how growing older can be absolutely divine. Now as I age, a part of me can say, "I lived there once, too."

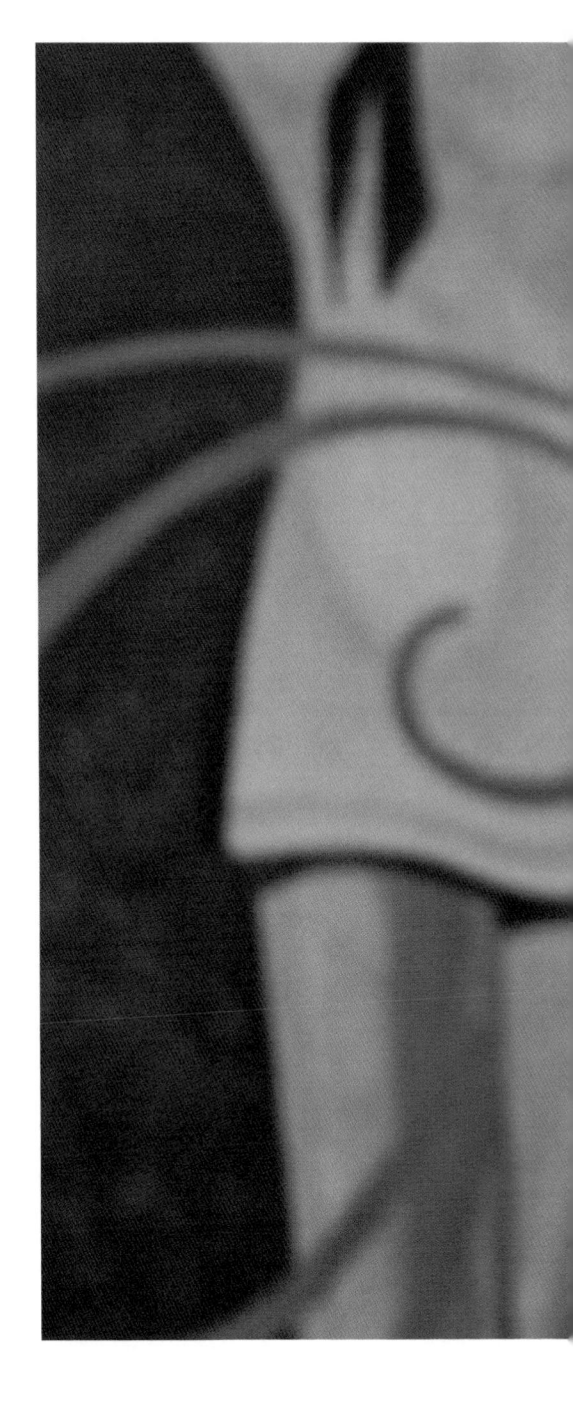

*Even with a face partially covered,
French women exude a beauty.
The mask adds to their mystery.*

It is incredibly difficult to ask a man in Paris to pose for a photo without it sounding like an invitation to something else—they are very forward. So I opted for this shot of great shoes heading for the Opera metro station. It was one of the two days it rained during my trip.

Men } Day 8 ~ April 28

It was raining today, and yet I saw the most impeccable outfit. Knee-length trench flopping lightly open, a navy cashmere sweater, a light gray scarf knotted around the neck, tailored black jeans, and the most glorious pair of (what had to be) Italian pointy, patent black shoes. It was on a man. Not a man like those with questionable orientation whose hips can fit into one leg of my jeans. A real man with broad shoulders who will get sweaty and change a tire. There he was, all shiny and looking amazing. I thought I passed him about eighteen times, and then I realized they were everywhere. All ages, all types of dress. Just as remarkable as the women. True, you get your scruffy ones every now and then. I can also spot the American man in the crowd in his polo-button-down-basic-T-shirt and sneakers from Wal-Apparel-wife-picked-them-out-mall. Here, I'm passing dozens of men's clothing stores with affordable styles I've never seen in the States. Coming out of those stores, carrying their own bags, are French men. Clearly they are shopping for themselves. With so many options around every corner, they are certainly able to find something that perfectly suits. Why do men in the United States have so few options comparably? Or is it merely their choices that are limiting them? Regardless, I could never see another baggy polo shirt tucked into pleated khakis and live happily ever after.

Wedding } Day 9 ~ April 29

Here comes the bride! Today Prince William married Kate, and what better way for a Canadian citizen in Paris to watch a royal wedding, than in an English Pub. But of course! I found myself a nice pub called the *Frog et Rosbif,* in the 2e, and made reservations for a table for one. The bar was filled with ex-British-pats from all over the globe, and as you can probably guess, mostly women except for the handful of guys who were dragged there (or into some other kind of drag). There was even a dog or two. It was enjoyable to speak English after a few days of struggling in French, and it was fun to reminisce about where we all were for the last two royal weddings of Diana and Fergie. I remember being up with my mom to watch Diana's wedding when it came on at 5 a.m. in Canada. I was ten and we had tea. Today, I ordered fish and chips and a pint, and I was reminded of my age, when a girl from California said, "I wasn't born yet." Nevertheless, the event was a hoot. We all cheered when the carriage pulled into view. We all became silent as we watched them exchange vows. In the ceremony it was asked, "Can any man provide just cause why these two should not be married?" More than half the bar called out their intentions to marry William, followed up by the male bartender shouting Monty Python-style, "He said any man!" Classic British humor. The bar erupted with laughter. All of us far from home, and yet finding something in common. We had all come to watch the hope of love.

Reflections }A PERMANENT ALIEN

Wherever I travel, in addition to having my luggage, camera, and pen, I also take with me the eyes of a Canadian Daughters of the American Revolution (DAR) American in Paris. I was born in Calgary in western Canada and lived there until I was nineteen. That last winter, after six weeks of minus 60°—not including the wind-chill factor—I decided to head south to go to college. I needed to defrost, and I was fearful I'd never meet anyone while wearing a ski mask nine months of the year. I headed south into the States. I've now lived in the United States just over half my life, obtaining residency through a permanent green card because my grandparents were American.

A Permanent Alien } ...continued

I've also traced my lineage back to Jacob G. Klock—a senator in New York during the American Revolution. So in addition to being a Canadian–American, I'm also an official DAR member—a group of historically focused women each one of us related to someone who fought in or supported the Revolution.

Knowing where I've come from, and having lived in many places, I feel like I live up to what it says on my green card. I'm a "permanent resident alien." I see and compare everything as if I'm from there and here (both in time and place) at the same time. I'm permanently on the go, while residing in other places, and so that makes me feel like an alien most of the time (minus the antennae).

As a Canadian in Paris, my first impression was about how ancient Paris was compared to my hometown. Calgary began as a North West Mounted Police outpost in 1876. By that time, Paris was already over 2,000 years old, and Baron Haussman under the rule of Napoleon III had just completed a massive renovation of the city. The wide, long-running boulevards, Arch de Triomph, elaborate bridges, expansive parks, and monument- or fountain-filled traffic circles were all part of a restructuring plan to make Paris more secure, more sanitary, and simply more beautiful.

Beautiful is an understatement. It's extraordinary. Expansive. Light-filled. Gilded gold. Clean. Glorious. Resplendent.

The Paris of today is much like Haussman's Paris of the 1870s. Very few of the monuments, buildings, or boulevards have changed, only their contents. It was such an incredibly brilliant plan that many cities, including Chicago, London, and Moscow tried to imitate it, but Paris did it on a grand scale. Despite the fact that most buildings in Paris are only six or seven stories tall, the neo-classic façades of massive stone, sculpted marble, friezes, and gilded domes made me feel so small—like Alice in Wonderland after swallowing the contents from the bottle labeled "Drink me." And we Canadians already feel insecure most of the time.

Our insecurity comes from living so close to the rebel Americans. As Robin Williams said, "Canada's like a loft apartment over a really great party." It's modern and beautiful up there, but America is the happening place. Aside from the weather, it's why I headed south and I love living here. But sometimes, while in Paris, being able to say I was from Canada had its rewards, because Americans and the French have had a strange, and sometimes estranged, relationship.

Without France's support during the Revolution, Americans might not have gained independence and could still be speaking the Queen's English. Without U.S. support during WWII, France might not have been liberated from the Nazis and they'd all be speaking German. In the state Capitol building in Richmond, Virginia, the room containing the busts of all the presidents from Virginia, also contains the bust of Lafayette, the French commander who helped America in the Revolution. In Paris, I came across a statue of Jefferson that was just unveiled in 2006, and a George Washington statue marks the beginning of the Avenue du President on the right bank. The French and Americans have each spent significant time with Ben Franklin, and each reveres him equally.

The United States and France are tied together and yet over the years, the relationship has been on-again, off-again (mostly off when that smart-aleck boy from Texas held office for eight years). How many Americans who have traveled abroad have said the French are rude? How many French have said the same thing about American visitors? I kind of liken the French–American relationship to how you feel about the guy that you lost your virginity to after you break up. You had a few life-altering moments together, and although he's been kind of a jerk since then, you can't help but have some affinity for him.

So, sometimes saying I live in the United States brought positive comments about how fun and youthful we are. Sometimes it did not. When my response of "I live in the United States" clearly brought up noses wrinkling with disgust, I'd throw in, "But I'm from Canada." I guess it brings up images of Niagara Falls, Rocky Mountains, overly polite people who can still fight over a hockey game, and some appreciation for the fact that we have adopted (some say butchered) French as one of our two official languages.

But there is some love for Americans by many, many French people. I found it in spades within the DAR. Just east of that George Washington statue, along the Seine, is a three-story statue of Lafayette. A gift from the United States, it was erected in coordination with the DAR in 1900. Now, if you think, as I did, that the DAR has a long way to reach across the ocean to Paris, think again. While the National Society of the DAR helped to erect that statue, today there is a DAR chapter in Paris. The Rochambeau Chapter has been an official DAR chapter since 1834. It's remarkable to think that I—a liberal Canadian from the British Commonwealth—am a DAR, but how many ex-patriots could there be in France?

A Permanent Alien } ...continued

During my stay, two of the Rochambeau Chapter members hosted me to an afternoon tea. Through their eyes, you would never know there had been any strain between the two nations. The French memory for their role in our Revolution is so strong that about 70 percent of their members are French—descendents from French soldiers who traversed the ocean to fight with Lafayette. Each year, this chapter still supports wreath-laying ceremonies at American cemeteries near Paris. Before I left our tea, they marked my Paris map with all the U.S. statues and showed me the best places to see Paris through the eyes of DAR.

Whenever I have traveled or lived somewhere, at some point I go in search of something that recognizes the tie we have to one another, in the hopes it will make me feel less like a visitor, so I'll be a better visitor. With their map-markings in hand, I rode out one afternoon to find that Lafayette statue, and discovered that it was erected by American children.

If school children across the ocean in 1900 can show their gratefulness, then I most certainly could show it while I was in Paris. Ugly American, please be gone. Let my French be less Canadian and more Parisian. Let me be gracious to my elders in historic Paris. Let this DAR remember those French ancestors who helped us gain independence. Let me act like a grateful permanent resident alien, even here.

And just in case you're wondering where Parisians might go to feel most like a Canadian, it's right near Notre Dame. There's a little place along the Left Bank of the Seine called the Great Canadian Pub. Naturally, they feel most like us while drinking our beer, eh? Hosers.

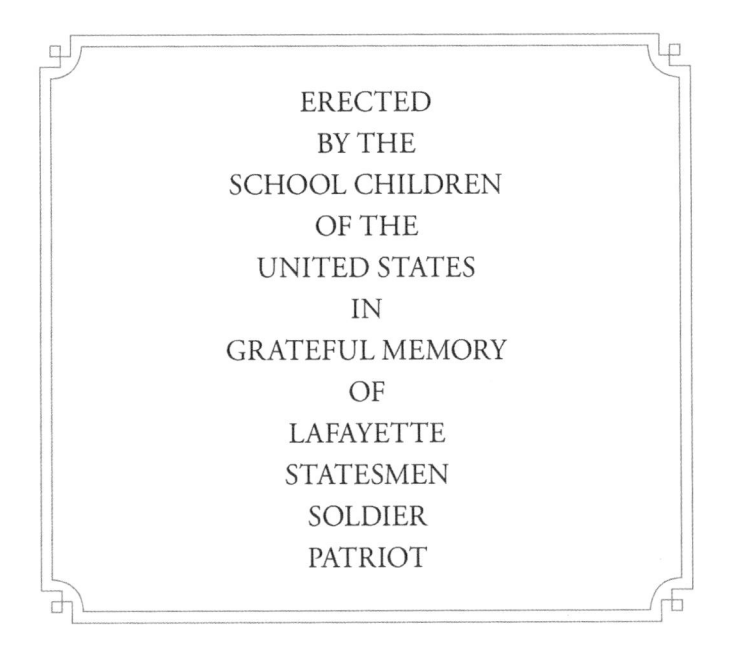

ERECTED
BY THE
SCHOOL CHILDREN
OF THE
UNITED STATES
IN
GRATEFUL MEMORY
OF
LAFAYETTE
STATESMEN
SOLDIER
PATRIOT

The view from the Wall of Peace, looking through the glass partitions that surround it. The glass is etched with signs of peace in forty-nine languages and eighteen alphabets.

Eiffel Tower } Day 10 ~ April 30

Tourists abound in Paris. And in no other place are they (we) more prolific than around the Eiffel Tower. It's a national landmark, built in honor of the World's Fair held here in 1889 commemorating the centenary of the French Revolution. Websites, guidebooks, tours, and the museum near the top of the tower provide all of the facts and details surrounding it, but it is the feeling of the whole area that left a greater impression upon me. Under the shadow of that sculpture and the trees, upon the green grass, I sat with families of various nationalities, generations, and genders playing and picnicking with their children. Couples napped together holding hands, making me miss Ted. Dogs romped and played. I helped take photos for strangers so they could be together in their photo (one of my favorite things to do on vacation), and a smiling couple helped take one of me. Some people sat quietly alone just taking it all in. Approximately 7 million visitors come here each year, and it's impossible to count how many countries could be represented at any given moment. At the foot of the tower is a newer monument built in 2000 called the Wall for Peace, which was inspired by the Wailing Wall. People can insert messages of peace into the chinks in the wall. After they do, many walk the distance to the tower, across the lawn of the *Parc du Champs de Mars*. If they stop, even for an instant, and simply look around them, they will see something remarkable. They will see what I saw:

Their wish has come true.

For all walks of life are there together.

Just being.

At peace.

Together.

Markets } Day 11 ~ May 1

I've been searching for the perfect word to sum up the French outdoor markets I've visited. The only one I came up with was "supercalifragilisticexpiale*delicious*." The sights! The color! The sounds! The smells! The food! Wait... let me slow down... I'll see if I can do it justice. Picture this: As if it's all a choreographed dance, the tables and wares are artfully arranged, the shoppers elegantly wheel their handcarts or strollers up and around, the stall owners move to and fro, and euros leap from hand-to-hand. The colors put Crayola® to shame—from the brown, dusty crusts of raisin bread, to the most vibrant, red radish, bright blue and gold rings, or purple linen scarf. There are men shouting, "*Poisson!*" while the women haggle for hats, flowers, or sausages, and children munch on carrots. The smell of fresh chickens roasting to perfection combines with hand-milled lavender soaps, and grilling garlic, so that the dogs at your feet drool and whimper along with you. Blue cheeses heaped upon goat cheeses are stacked at stalls next to those with fat heads of broccoli and white asparagus. *Macarons* are piled with precision. Olives nestle in oil swimming with red peppers. Rustic, white, brown, cream, and green sauces lie in great vats waiting for you. Calling sweetly to you. It makes me wish I had nine lives so I could come back again. And again. Again. Again. Again. Again. Again. And then just once more, so I may try it all.

*Baskets of mushrooms, garlic, and herbs
are among the items in the markets
adding to a heavenly, heady aroma, and
the beautiful displays of bounty.*

7th SAXE-BRETEUIL MARKET

{ ...cupcakes, bread, fish, produce, eggs ... }

{ ...fresh, delicious, tasty, colorful... }

Reflections } FIT FOR FOOD

Nearly every day of my five weeks in France I drank coffee loaded with cream and sugar for breakfast and had a glass or a half carafe of wine with lunch or dinner. I ate croissants or pastries in the morning and bread with every meal, and cheese made a showing on my plate sometimes twice a day. I made special excursions to find the best *macarons*, the sweetest chocolate (Café Viennes for the chocolate *chaud*), and the crustiest *crème brûlée* (Café des Modernes). Crepes, ice cream, cakes, custards, pastries, candies—I hardly ever missed a dessert. It was like unleashing a sleeping dragon. All of the color, all of the richness of flavors, all of the glorious foooooooood.

Fit for Food } ...continued

And yet I dropped five pounds and I've never felt better or healthier since I was a kid.

Anyone who has read *French Women Don't Get Fat* or *Entré Nous: A Woman's Guide to Finding Her Inner French Girl* can delve deeply into how the French can live so fully at the table and stay so slim. So I won't go into it that much again, except to say, it's all true. I was taking longer to eat—sometimes up to three hours for the same meal it would have taken twenty minutes to eat in my kitchen at home. The portions were smaller. There was little to no processed food. Aside from sweets and liquor, my meals were mostly fresh veggies and fruits, fish, meats, and breads, mostly from local farms and producers within one hundred miles of Paris. I was also on my feet for hours and hours and miles and miles a day.

I've always said that if you want to figure out where exactly those "really comfortable shoes" you bought are going to start giving you trouble, you could just walk around New York and your feet will find the spot. The same is true of Paris. Whenever I wasn't writing at a café, eating, or sleeping, I was on the move. If not on foot, by bike. One day I walked from the Eiffel Tower to my apartment. That was about four miles. It doesn't seem like much, but that morning I first biked to an early morning market. Then I walked to lunch. Shopped in the afternoon, wrote while I

was at lunch and breakfast, and then after returning to my apartment to freshen up, I walked to dinner. According to my calculations, my total caloric output that day was just over 2,000. Given my average eating habits while I was there, I figure my input was about 1,500. As Ted often tells his therapy patients who are struggling with weight issues, "If the input exceeds the output, it stays put." My output exceeded the input. So it went kaput.

The most notable difference, however, was the simple fact that not once in five weeks did I think about caloric intake or expenditure figures affecting my figure. *Not once.* All of the above calculations were gathered upon returning home to calorie-obsessed America. (Ironically, the same country where forty-nine states have an obesity rate over 30 percent.) Here, my inbox fills with reminders from WebMD.com and RealAge.com to eat healthy, cut down, or cut out everything I coveted in France. Here, menus at restaurants tell me how many calories are in each dish. To help me? Shock me? Direct my choices with guilt? Here, magazine ads tell me I can lose unwanted pounds by actually paying for prepared or processed meals, popping pills, or tracking my every move on my new phone app. Ahhhhh! Come on! I want to enjoy life. Shuuut uuuup already!

It was so simple there. The lifestyle I had for five weeks was guilt-free and made me slimmer simply because I was moving around and eating a common-sense diet. So good-bye weight, and hello tight ass. By the time Ted arrived on Day 30, he took one look at my toned calves and thighs in a skirt and said, "Look at those! Where did you get those?" Yes, I was touring and visiting, which made all the walking easier. But I also wrote. A lot. You can't walk and write at the same time. But in between the lines, I was moving. Fast. Not sauntering. Not strolling. Speed-walking like every good French woman who refuses to miss a metro train. Even in heels. My days were filled with creating, writing, cycling, photographing, walking, learning, loving, and experiencing.

Yes, food was a part of that experience, but it was not just fuel. It was an elegant, sweet, satisfying, intoxicating, tasteful experience to be savored, not shoveled into my system. The waiters expect you to slow it down and take your time. It was easy as pie (which I never once ate in Paris) to find a waiter to take my order, but it was three times as difficult to get them to bring the bill. They don't want to rush you. Stay. Taste it. Linger. Let it roll around on your plate and in your mouth so you remember how lovely it was. Then have dessert before you walk home.

The food was fresh. Bread with no preservatives, garden vegetables and fruits to make you swoon, hand-squeezed orange juice, and tap water considered some of the cleanest and best in the world. Between restaurants, the produce stands, the city-wide gorgeous water fountains, and the endless, massive, delectable markets, Paris should be called the city of food. Their approach to food should be adopted worldwide. Fresh. Flavorful. Fantastic. Easily available and affordable to the masses. A whole roasted chicken, new potatoes that have caught all the drippings, a kilo of lettuce, two large beef "boeuf" tomatoes, a bag of cherries, half a dozen farm eggs, a garlic clove bigger than my palm, a baguette, two breakfast croissants, and a block of walnut-crusted cheese cost me about $25 U.S. dollars, and I ate off it all for three days.

Upon returning home, I asked a Parisian friend who lives near me how she does it. How does she manage to adjust to our grocery stores and our food when she comes back from Paris? I was having a heck of a time with it. She shook her head sympathetically and said, "I remember one time I came back to the States. I went to the grocery store. I stood in the aisles. And I cried. I literally cried."

Once you awaken the sleeping dragon within your palette, and let him loose with no remorse, he cries. He literally cries when he is not properly fed.

Thoughout large department stores and covered markets, goods abound and people shop for treasures and inspiration.

{ *...sniffing, touching and examining...* }

Retail } Day 12 ~ May 2

A friend of mine told me before I left that retail is dead. He said, "You will still go somewhere for a service, but everyone is just going to buy their stuff online." He should have come to Paris. I couldn't turn down a street, even if it felt like an alleyway, without running into some store that sells some small select grouping of things that I didn't know was a thing. To my friend's credit, I think what is helping those retailers is their location. They are in the midst of service stores, bakeries, butchers, cafés, apartments, offices, bookstores, and other you-name-it shops. They're all working together in clumps, so they all work. The other notable fact for retail success in Paris is that people obviously still like to touch stuff. You should see the people of Paris poking, smelling, pulling, and pushing the stuff around like blind kleptomaniacs. Over the last several days—even on weekdays—I've seen so many people out shopping and fingering the merchandise that I've wondered if anyone in Paris actually works for a living. Certainly, they are having a lovely time buying local. And so am I. I've begun sniffing, touching, and examining all kinds of objects in tiny little stores the size of my guest bathroom back home. Here, department stores are impressive, too—gorgeous, elaborate, and eye-catching—but I've found the bargains and the people most willing to engage are in a little business for themselves.

Bread } Day 13 ~ May 3

Don't worry if you trip and fall while touring Paris, because you'll land on a loaf of bread. It's in restaurants with every meal. It walks by you in the hands of adults and children—Parisians prefer to sit and enjoy a leisurely meal, but the baguette is a favorite walking food. As for the places that sell bread, called boulangeries, they are everywhere. Don't believe me? Just type in *"Boulangerie* Paris" in Google maps. Every dot is considered a *boulangerie.* The generally accepted method for identifying the best *boulangerie* is the one closest to your home, so the bread will actually make it to your flat before you have eaten it. Always, it should be purchased for the next meal. French law dictates that a true French baguette should contain only flour, yeast, salt, and water. Beyond the baguette, there are so many types of bread here. It's no wonder they're right around each and every corner. All this doughy goodness is quite a change for me. I was so careful before I left home to watch my bread intake, avoiding carbs, wheat, and all things white. But here, with all the walking I'm doing, I say screw it. I'm happily swimming in a gluten-enriched life. With each crunchy, air-filled bite, I'm finding that it's okay to let myself simply enjoy tearing off a piece of life to relish in the sweet and savory experience while it's fresh. I'm grabbing a loaf for today knowing tomorrow is another fabulous bread day.

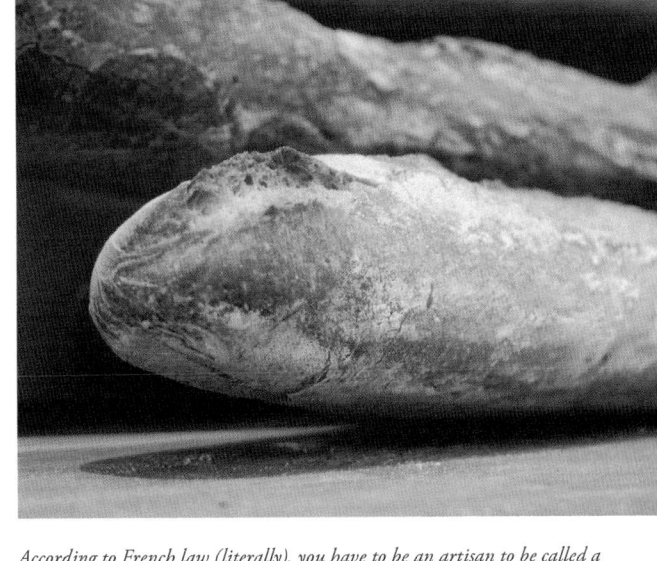

According to French law (literally), you have to be an artisan to be called a baker. It's so important, some shops are called "Boulangerie Artisan," so you can be twice as certain. Artisans abound at the annual bread festival held in May. Here, bread dough is creatively formed into a face before baking.

Apartment } Day 14 ~ May 4

I'm so glad I chose to stay in an apartment instead of a hotel. I feel like I have a home to return to after my wanderings, and it is also a little peek into the French daily life. A second-floor walk-up, mine is a small, cozy flat that is uncluttered and clean. I have my own kitchen, and I like the apartment's subtle details. There are pieces of Limoges china in the cabinet (keep in mind this is someone's *rental* property). The gorgeous gold wallpaper is not actually paper, it is padded jacquard fabric, and the ceiling is linen. There's a charming fold-top desk where I write each night before I go deal with my pillow. You see, there is a strange, long, wiener-shaped pillow on my bed. It's as long as I am tall and has the diameter of a large dinner plate. It's very squishy. And I have no idea how I'm supposed to sleep with it. Each night the thing and I wrestle around a bit trying to figure out how best to share the bed. Do I leave it along the top and put my head in the middle of the long section? Should I be on my back, but with it scrunched down over my shoulders? Lay alongside it? Mostly I wake up straddling it in a way that makes both the pillow and me uncomfortable. There is one other pillow, but it's about two-feet square and so soft I can feel the mattress through it. Regardless, I'm enjoying my home away from home with the view of the treetops, and I'm sure I'll get the hang of that bolster-style pillow eventually. But they should really throw it out after I leave.

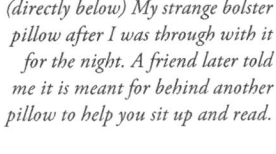

(directly below) My strange bolster pillow after I was through with it for the night. A friend later told me it is meant for behind another pillow to help you sit up and read.

(bottom) This antique mirror reflects the writing desk where I composed most of the journal. Tall seven-foot windows opened to let in the beautiful 70° breezes.

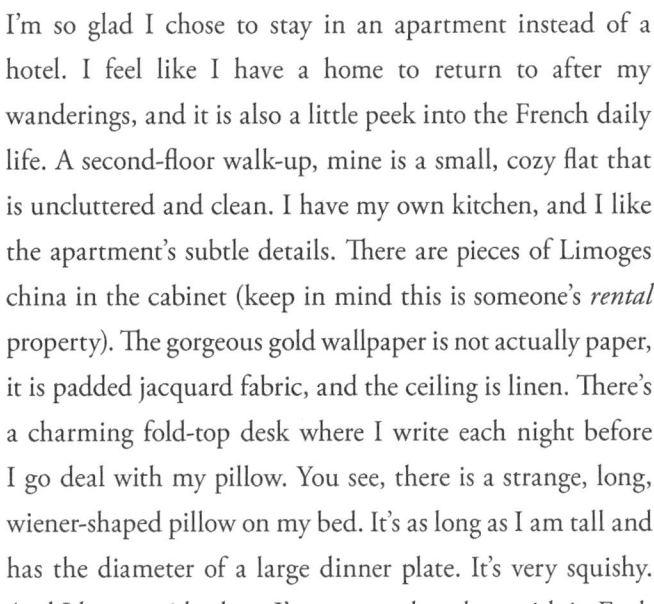

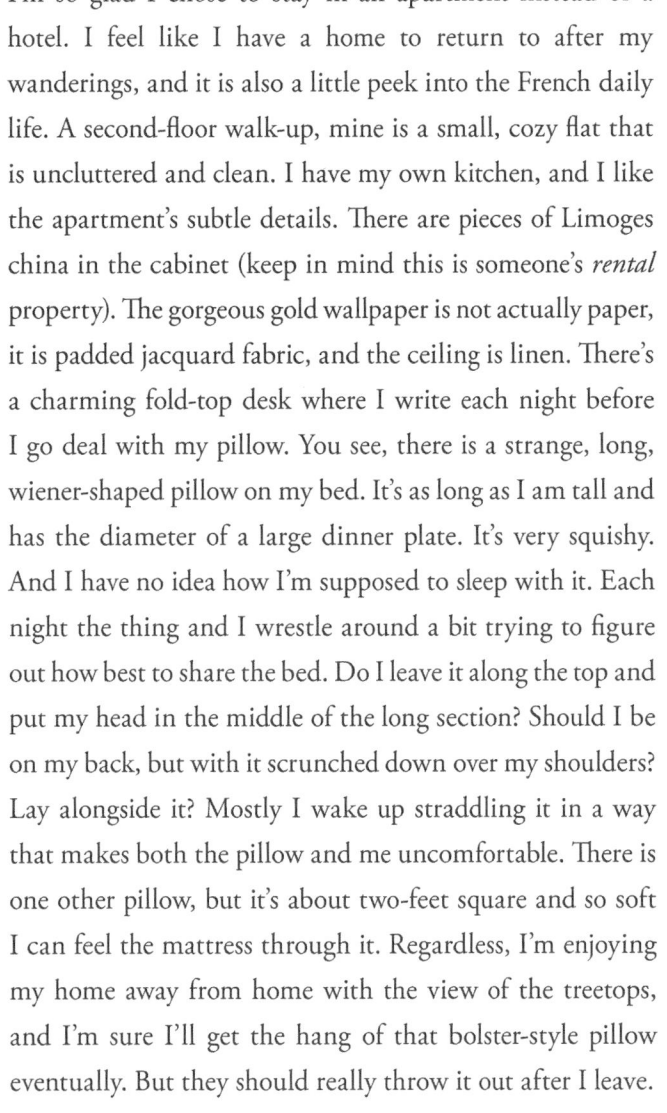

Lost } Day 15 ~ May 5

I got lost. Hopelessly, wonderfully, nowhere in particular-ly lost. I did start out my day with a planned visit to a museum, but once I left it I just got wanderlust for the next *eight* hours. It sounds frightening, but no, wandering in Paris is delightful. Every corner I went around had another little strip of charming stores, grand statues, festive cafés, gardens, architecture, flowers, or monuments to behold. With no phone, and limited email access, being unplugged is giving me the freedom to go out for these aimless excursions whenever writing hits a wall or my curiosity gets the best of me. My favorite spots are the really small, short streets that wind together in a jumbled, crooked mess. There, the traffic noise is reduced significantly, the shopkeepers are a bit friendlier, the wares are more unique, and cafés are quainter. It's there that Paris feels more like Paris. In my meandering, I tried to visit the overcrowded Arc de Triomphe and ended up on the Champs Élysées yesterday. Within about five minutes, I grabbed a bicycle and escaped the area entirely. I didn't come to Paris to see tourists eating fast food and buying overpriced American designer clothing. It isn't the romantic boulevard it was when Joni Mitchell sang about it. My footsteps finally led me to the crab shack and bar at the end of my block. It is fast becoming a favorite. It is managed by Bandit-the-dog who barks at everything he's never seen before and sits next to me begging for food. Dorothée, his owner, speaks wonderful English, so here I can learn and share equally. We chat until she closes for the night. As my day of wandering ended, words from that same Joni Mitchell song come to me: "I was a free man in Paris, I felt unfettered and alive. There was nobody calling me up for favors, and no one's future to decide…"

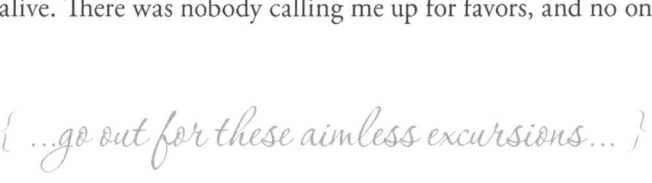

{ …go out for these aimless excursions… }

Writers } Day 16 ~ May 6

There is a great history of writers who have lived, worked, or visited Paris, and the city is very proud of this heritage. Victor Hugo, Hemingway, Gertrude Stein, James Joyce, and many others all spent time here crafting feelings into words. I feel quite a responsibility to do wonderful things with my work, and plenty of inspiration should I hit a wall. Which I did. I had been planning, organizing, and writing for weeks before I came, and upon arrival, I watched a blank screen for a couple of days. Then I went to a little store on the Left Bank (which they should call the South Bank, but "nothing is simple in Paris," I've been told). Shakespeare and Company is an English-only bookstore spilling forth novelists, poets, and other writers for more than sixty years. It smells a little funny, but the bindings, the titles, the readers, and the opportunity to become one of those contained in the shelves are mesmerizing. The upstairs is a reading library. I use the term "library" loosely, for you can't take out the books and it's set up like no library I've ever seen. Everything up there is as heaped, crooked, and lovingly explored like the little Paris streets. The books sit alongside worn chairs, old typewriters, a piano, and a children's nook. I've visited it a couple times since I've been here, and will grace its doorway again, because the history is palpable, the staff delightful, and the collection incredibly moving. Going there made me reach down deep and find the words in my internal alcove. I owe it to all those who have come before me to keep writing. To keep writing alive. And yes, despite owning and using a Kindle, I still buy books. Five so far this trip.

The upstairs lending library at Shakespeare and Company is not a disappointment. Parisians love books and bookstores, and they are almost as numerous as the boulangeries. *My Kindle is quite a curiosity in this city.*

Another favorite bookstore I frequented was the Abbey Bookstore. It's a fabulous Canadian bookstore with free coffee with maple syrup. Book reading events are hosted outside for there simply isn't room among the pages inside. Here, the cellar is filled to overflowing.

Reflections }SHAKESPEARE AND COMPANY

I went to the Mad Hatter's Tea Party at Shakespeare and Company. It was because of Hilary that I went. Or was it because of Worth? Maybe it was Hemingway. But that would mean it was because of Sylvia Beach. She owned the bookstore almost seventy-five years ago, thirty-five years before I was born. So that can't be it. It's not because of George Whitman either, for we've never met. In actuality, I think it was my own circumstances that led me there. In my preparations for my trip to write in Paris, I was reading many books about writing and Paris. Tour-guide books, travel logs, memoirs, and naturally *A Moveable Feast*. Enter Ernest Hemingway.

Shakespeare & Co. } ...continued

Hemingway had been in Paris in the 1930s, writing of course, and thankfully for fans, writers, book-lovers, and Parisians, before he died in 1964, he wrote about his adventures. Published posthumously, *A Moveable Feast* allows the reader to wander the streets of Paris and places that still exist. We enter into the author's mind as he bets at the track, gambles on writing, and hangs around with the likes of Ezra Pound, F. Scott Fitzgerald, Gertrude Stein, and a cast of literal literary characters.

Within Hemingway's pages, I was introduced to Sylvia Beach. She began and owned the English bookstore and lending library in Paris called Shakespeare and Company, originally in the 6th arrondissement. As-yet-famous authors, all of them struggling to get their written word read by somebody (anybody), mingled with the well-published. She published James Joyce for the first time and forged an opportunity for authors to discuss literature, read others, and hopefully see their own books on a shelf. Fascinated by the story, I discovered that the store ended up expanding to 12 rue de l'Odéon in 1921, but was forced to close after the fall of Paris to the Germans in 1941. Sylvia was interned. She kept her books hidden in a vacant apartment, but the store never reopened. Deflated, I wondered where on earth all of us writers were supposed to meet in Paris now.

A week after reading about the closing, an old friend named Worth came to visit us. Yes, it is a fabulous name, and Worth lives up to it, for he is one of the most valuable men you shall ever meet. He has moved four blocks in sixty-five years, but has seen more of the world than all my friends and the last eight presidents combined. There is no need to speak around Worth. He never dominates a conversation, but a simple question like, "where have you been lately," will prompt a jaw-dropping story about a country and a people you didn't know existed that he can delightfully describe for half an hour. On this particular visit, he discovered my impending trip to Paris and, knowing my love of the written word, said to me, "there is the best little bookstore in all the world in Paris… I think it's still there… it's been years since I was there… but you have to go… you can't buy the books upstairs, you can only read them… but oh, it's called…"

"…Shakespeare and Company," we both said.

With furry eyebrows raised with delight, he said, "You've heard of it! You have to go. It's out of this world!" It's not an often-used phrase with Worth, but given how much of the world he has seen, when he says something is "out of this world," I completely believe him. I promised I would visit the store.

A couple of weeks before the trip, I researched the store online and sent them an inquiry. I was on the hunt for another copy of Hemingway's book and thought I would take a chance on Shakespeare and Company having one. Enter Hilary who works at the store. Within a couple of days, she emailed me to say they had one and would set it aside. Fast forward to arriving in Paris. Not wanting to put them out, or risk losing my held copy, I made my way to the Left Bank to find Hilary within a day or two after arriving. With a view of Notre Dame, behind a glorious green water fountain, amid old leather suitcases filled with on-sale books outside, I found the old store and stepped inside.

I don't think you can call this simply a bookstore. It is a delightfully wild land of literary abandonment and insanity—a page-filled palace overflowing with words, phrases, novels writers, readers, and inspiration. Every wall, shelf, table, stair, and ceiling runs at an unnatural angle, height, or length to everything else. It smells a little like dust, book-binder's glue, body odor, and rose water. In tattered chairs, on piano benches (next to a piano that anyone can play), on the stairs, and on crates are hunched-over bookworms with their noses deep in pages, keeping to themselves with delight. Strange, quaint signs in English are wedged into spaces along with typewriters, framed photos, and one hell of a collection of books. New books are on the first floor, and treasured and well-loved on the second. The

Shakespeare & Co. } ...continued

checkout desk, slightly obscured from the door, is tucked in a corner behind bulletins and patrons as if it, too, would hate to intrude on your reading. It was there in that little front nook that I met Hilary. She turned out to be Canadian, like me, and told me she'd landed a job in the best bookstore in the world three years ago and could not believe her luck. She also asked me if I'd heard about the Mad Hatter's Tea Party hosted by the owner.

Enter George Whitman. He had known Sylvia Beach, and in 1951 he opened a bookstore on the Left Bank called *Les Mistral*. After Sylvia died, he changed the name of his shop in her honor. This revived Shakespeare and Company once again lives and is still owned by George. Still a lending library and a bookstore like Sylvia's was, when George reopened in the 1950s, it overflowed with beat-writers of the period. Anyone willing to lend a hand cleaning up the place could, for a spell, hang around, sleep overnight, or sometimes even run the store. Those who did were dubbed Tumbleweeds. Much of the feeling that George brought to the place, is still there today, as is George. As of this writing, he is about ninety-seven, and he has retired to his apartments upstairs. His daughter, Sylvia, named after the original owner, is running it now. One of the crazy things that George carried over from Sylvia is the Mad Hatter's Tea Party, to which Hilary had casually extended me an invitation.

To attend this delightful event, I simply needed to hear about it. I did not need an invitation. There was no list for my name to be on. I needed only the knowledge of when and where it occurred. An unadvertised event, it happens every week at roughly the same time, if the person running it is able to come. It used to be George. Now, his longtime friend, Panmelis—a poet and painter—comes each week to run it for him.

So one Sunday, I joined the party. One-by-one we trickle upstairs from the store to the small room that is George's front living room. Bookshelves line the crooked, dusty walls and are crammed with worn copies of favorite novels and authors, pictures of George and fellow writers or travelers, and notebooks that document all of the Tumbleweeds who have worked the shelves temporarily. A picture of Walt Whitman hangs near the door, and it rumbles through the group that George used to say they were related. A typewriter sits abandoned on a pile of books under the small, open window, and a new 21″ Macintosh monitor sits on the old wooden desk. A sign over the door says, "Visitors welcome to the Museum of the Lost Generation." A bottomless teapot with a collection of cups as mismatched as those of us collecting in the room is brought out from the kitchen by Panmelis. Sugar cubes and cream are produced, and she begins the party.

It's like no other gathering. People are squished together on a twin bed pushed against a wall of mirrors to serve as a sofa. Strangers are sitting on the sagging mattress with their legs touching, instantly connecting them. Straight-backed chairs are produced out of nowhere, with many of us, including me, gathered around a weathered, round wooden table. The dozen or more of us are instructed to tell the group a bit about how we arrived at the party. We also write a few lines in a school-like notebook so Panmelis may read them later to George. The tales are wildly varied, and mine is among the most mundane.

A man, now in his fifties, says he came through in his thirties after a trip to Africa. George invited him to stay, and he slept in the twin bed upon which he now sat. They had talked of their world travels, George made him pancakes in the morning, and he had attended his first tea party. He had come back more than twenty years later in the hopes of finding George and a few Mad Hatters in a place that still looked familiar.

Another woman tells of a friend who had come to visit the shop many years earlier. The friend had asked George, working the corner cash desk, so many questions that eventually he stood and announced he was bored and was going to get a beer. "You'll run the desk while I'm gone," he said. The friend blanched and said she didn't know anything about running a bookshop. "The price is on the book, you take the Francs, and you give them change. It's not hard," he said. And he walked out the door in search of drink. The friend slipped behind the desk, became a Tumbleweed, and the woman sitting before us had been planning her trip ever since she had heard the tale.

For Panmelis, a fiery blond woman now probably in her seventies, her stories of George were just as legendary. Wanting to read her new poetry at weekly events, she had come as a young woman in the hopes of being added to the list of speakers at the bookstore. George reviewed her work and said, "This week. You'll come and read this week." With shaking hands from the short preparation time, she came as instructed, and it must have been that moment that bound her to George forever. When she speaks of him, it is with a fondness that softens her entire being, and you can feel her leave the room to a decade long ago. When she looks at old pictures of him around the parlor, she mumbles and laughs, "Just look at him. He simply has to live forever. Yes, I think he must go on living forever."

Shakespeare & Co. } ...continued

An hour into the two-hour party, Panmelis quickly stood and pointed at me. With her hand shaking, and her eyes bursting with excitement, she asked, "Do you have a poem in your pocket?" Bewildered, I shook my head. "A poem, a song maybe. You look like you could sing." I most certainly cannot. The rest of the room, save one or two returning guests, looked as surprised as I was.

Poem-in-your-pocket-time is when you share with the group poetry memorized, written by you or others, or even sung. It leads to the most marvelous discussions. For the next hour, we conversed on prose and poetry, and why we are compelled to write, as we travel through various places in the world. It ends when the sound of the bells of Notre Dame float through the small, open window over the typewriter. Slowly everyone descends into the store two stories below, many of us in clumps of two or three wanting to extend the conversation.

Later, as I walked alone toward my apartment, it occurred to me that this Mad Hatter's Tea Party actually serves to remove a bit of the madness from the world. I sometimes wonder where my collective choices—my partners and friends, life decisions, and travel paths—are leading me.

Now I know, at the very least, it leads to a small room over an ancient bookstore with strangers who together become part of its history. All of us in one room. A room with great intention.

Writers need a place to gather given how much time we spend alone in the worlds we create. In a French-speaking city filled with casual tourists, English-speaking world-travelers need a place to come where they can meet others afflicted with the same depth of wanderlust. For that brief time, we could all find a home in a foreign place. Our different paths brought us to sit leg to leg and share our stories over a cup of tea. The longevity of Shakespeare and Company is a wonderful net of assurance for each Mad Hatter. So when we are out writing or on another journey, we know where we can go, should we happen to fall through again.

Alone } Day 17 ~ May 7

This is the first time in a couple of years that I've traveled alone, without Ted, family, or a friend. It has its advantages at times. I've been enjoying my time to write until the wee hours, sit in parks with a book, fiddle with samples in makeup stores, or contemplate my forty-year-old pores in the mirror. When I really feel I am alone (aside from at night in the bedroom) is while seeing new things and during meals in restaurants. I like to share in experiences, and so I find myself wanting to grab Ted's arm and point at things. When I laughed at a comment on a museum tour, the woman next to me did not find it as funny as he would have. When I go out to eat, I do miss him more. When it comes to sharing food, Ted and I simply cannot help ourselves, and we'll often stab at each other's plates to experience twice as much. Alone though, waiters always look behind me to see whom I'm with before they seat me. "*Juste moi,*" I've come to say. Sometimes, it brings enough pity I get a great table, and extra nice service (or a flirtation or two). Once, it got me a crappy table next to the silverware and drink station, which resulted, literally, in clean knives being thrown over my head into the bin. I have also learned to take my Kindle while dining alone, because it's very hard to figure out where to look. If I look at the next table, which I do because I want to see what they've ordered, it's an intrusion on their meal. Clearly, watching the male waiter while I'm alone is out of the question, as that spot in my bed is reserved for Ted and my now very personal pillow.

Holiday } Day 18 ~ May 8

In Europe, short excursions to go "on holiday" to other countries are easy, fast, and affordable. For my birthday, my brother and sister-in-law surprised me with a train ticket to… London! So I booked the Chunnel and have come here to enjoy the sights and take a break from speaking French. Paris and London, only 2.5 hours apart by train, are such a world apart. The most remarkable difference is the people. The Brits are just so much dang fun! I don't know if it's because beer runneth over, or it's to compensate for the gray skies, but I now see where my silly Canadian humor began. The guffaws at nearby tables or during my interactions were also more noticeable to me because I realized I haven't heard anyone laugh that hard in Paris. I don't think I'll ever see a Frenchman spit wine out of his nose over a joke. They're far too serious. I'm different here, too. With no language barrier, I am so much funnier in London. In Paris, my red hair and pale complexion stand out and sometimes garner comments. In London, I look like every other pasty English girl. But that enables me to slide in, gawk, ask men for directions, and really chat it up with people. I am in love with Londoners. They are delightful, charming, polite, eager to pose for pictures, and honestly the best part of what is already a jolly good time.

{ *…a remarkable difference…* }

London	Paris
Bagpipes	Accordions
Shakespeare	Victor Hugo
Double-decker bus	Seine boat
Underground	Metro
Loo/WC for a fee	Toilettes for free
Pubs everywhere	Cafés everywhere
Italian coffee	French press
Dry toast with jam	French bread
Bells of Big Ben	Bells of Notre Dame
Eye contact	Keep to yourself
Clocks everywhere	Why be on time?
Smile easily	Look constipated

This little collection of figurines is part of the flower market near Notre Dame. In addition to plants and garden items, on Sundays it is also a bird market.

London } Day 19 ~ May 9

While in London, I have seen some of the usual suspects—Westminster Hall, Buckingham Palace, the River Thames—and had fish and chips in a pub with a pint, etc. With limited time, what I did was a lot of walking. I took a guided photo walking tour that enabled me to learn a bit about the city, and my camera. To let my feet rest, I bought a ticket to a 2.5-hour performance of a Shakespeare play in the Globe Theatre. Modeled after the original theater, the twenty-sided, thatched-roof, open-air experience made me feel like it was suddenly 1605. Continuing my trek across London, I also walked through the Notting Hill Portobello market (yes the one from the movie). In this two-mile antiques, goods, and produce market, I came to discover that the British understand the delicacy of things. Pocket watches have tiny engravings. A compass is a treasured item to hold or put atop a walking cane. And it was there among all the stuff, I found my grandmother. I'd been searching for a really great teapot after my last one unfortunately cracked. There in the midst of more than eight blocks of little tables, I turned and found one in stall no. 10 that looked so much like hers I nearly cried. With only £34 left in my pocket, and needing £4 for the tube ticket back to the train home, I bought her. It wasn't about buying a thing. It was about her memory.

She would have loved London, and so she showed up to be with me, I think. With only enough change for an orange juice and shortbread, I took that teapot and together with half of London, we snacked and napped in Kensington Gardens. And then we came home. Even the title of Shakespeare's play summed up my London excursion: *All's Well That Ends Well*. Now, back to Paris…

This is the teapot found in stall no. 10 in the Notting Hill Portobello Road Market, among other delightful English wares and cliché scenes.

Reflections } THROUGH MY LENS

If a picture is worth a thousand words, then I have over 2.1 million words from this trip, beyond those I actually wrote. Over 2,100 photographs from the month in France have been added to a collection of over 6,000 already on my laptop of family, friends, felines, and festivities. True, many are duplicates as I tried to get lighting or focus just right, and some aren't really usable at all because I got it wrong. But for the most part I feel good that the years of images, and certainly those from this journey, are a well-rounded collection of memories.

Through my lens } ...continued

I am by no means a professional photographer. It's a hobby, and it's probably my father's fault. He had an old Pentax, which still sits on my fireplace mantel in my office. I remember it being part of him, like a constant companion. The smell of the leather on the strap and the case. The sound of the film pushing into the canister with each wind to advance the frame. The bulky tripod. His one eye winked shut to see us through the viewfinder. He shared his love with me, showed me a bit about how his camera worked, and encouraged me in the hobby, and so over the years it developed (pun intended) into a love for photography of my own. Now my own Canon Rebel® is my companion in capturing the adventures.

Part of me takes photographs as a way to prove things happened. It's as if, after I come home from vacation, it's hard to believe I was actually there. Was that me? Did I see that? Did we do that? Short stays are even more fleeting in the memory, and so knowing my stay in London would be brief—a whirlwind forty hours at most—I included a photo walking tour in my plans.

I've taken such tours before in other cities where time is limited. You get history and a great walk, you see major highlights, and you go home with pictures that have most likely turned out because you're with a professional. With my photos, it's about learning the craft and working to improve, too. So I get the added bonus of someone walking with me who knows my camera better than I do.

It's important to get to know my camera, because it's like having a third eye along on the trip. And in London, I really felt like I needed that because there is so *bloody* much to see! That third eye, allowed me to capture forty hours of little moments into about two hundred or so "paintings," that I could easily transport home. A collection of antique rugby balls, worn valises, and old pool cues at the Portobello Road market became a still life with my aperture set on 5.0. With it set on 9.0, a beautiful view of two cranes sunning on a rock

in the middle of the pond with Buckingham Palace in the background became a landscape. By learning how to let more light into the foreground, I was able to capture all of the laugh-lines on the sweet, smiling man near Notting Hill, and he became a portrait. By slowing down the shutter speed, the spinning motion of a carousel on the South Bank made the photo look more like Monet's *Water Lilies* than a snapshot of a merry-go-round.

Time is another of the beautiful things the camera allows me to stop. And Londoners love time. Hundreds of public clocks can be seen in London, with Big Ben being the most photographed. I've never seen so many in one place. While in Paris, no one cares if you are on time, here there is a constant reminder of it ticking by. (Hmmm. Maybe that's why the Brits drink so much.) During my abbreviated stay, my camera bought me time in two ways. It turned out I was the only one on the walking tour, so my guide graciously turned my two-hour excursion into four. It also bought it by simply slowing it down. In the midst of walking briskly from Buckingham Palace, through the gardens, and over past Parliament, I had to stop, pay attention, and then take every opportunity that came to freeze the frame in front of me through that single lens. It made my trip more memorable. It took home some lovely photographs of both the North and South Banks, Shakespeare's theater,

double-decker buses, Kensington Gardens, several lovely English faces, amazing market wonders, and the inside of a pub, naturally. I felt like I really got to *see* London. Sure my feet were exhausted, but my eyes were delighted.

In addition to my captured moments, I took back to Paris a desire for better timing. Until now, I had been sliding in with the rest of Paris, staying up late and sleeping in. But for a photographer, it's all about finding the right light, and the best time for that is early morning or late evening. I can look at photos now and tell you approximately what time of day they were taken. Many of mine from the first two weeks were taken between 10 a.m. and 4 p.m. That had to change.

So that's when I set aside a few times to capture Paris at sunrise and sunset. Paris is a nighttime city and so no photo collection would be complete without a shot that captures the flicker and the traffic. Early evening brings the ultraviolet blues and purples, paving the streets with lavender and platinum. But her mornings are devoid of the noise. At sunrise, the city is naked, stripped down, still resting to gear up before another metropolitan, tourist-filled day. The layout of the streets, and the glorious Seine and bridges wake up with her as she becomes the city of morning light. The air is still cool and clear, the only sounds are of the occasional

Through my lens } ...continued

café opening up or a street cleaner going by. Sunrise brings the glorious red end of the light spectrum, which in Paris makes the stone of the buildings glow as if they are painted with gold.

It was then, cycling across her streets with my camera over my shoulder, that I realized it was in my going off to capture the city on film, that I am capturing internal memories. The memory of me gliding down the empty Champs Élysées, light just barely touching each leaf of each tree, the morning breeze tugging at my hair—it is a feeling that is photographed within me. As if the memories are taken like photos in multiple-shot bursts, I can visually pull up every frame of that single adventure so they run together like a film in slow motion. Riding. Soaring. Free. Peddling. Living. Moving. Creative. Awake. Wonderful, happy memories. I have so many of them.

If I take all of the images that are on my laptop from this trip, all of the others going all the way back to 2007, and I add it to the images I have on backup hard drives, DVDs, or film, I estimate I've about 15,000 images so far in this life. In another forty years that may double to become 30,000. What on earth am I going to do with them all?

Years ago, a friend in his thirties told me he didn't watch TV because he knew at some point in his life he'd be old and stuck in a single bed in a nursing home. In the meantime, he was out making memories while his body and mind kept up. Once they began to wither, he could sit in his one old chair and watch *Friends* and believe all the episodes were new. I see now what he meant.

When my memory is fading, and I am bound to a single room, perhaps I will sit before an ancient (solar-powered) Apple laptop and my arthritic hand will scroll through these 15,000 images and those yet to be taken. They will help me remember a life filled with experiences rather than things. With people and pets I loved, and who loved me during my life behind the lens. Frame by frame by wonderful, sad, moving, delightful, thrilling, loving, memorable frame. Certainly they may help me remember my time in London. And I can hopefully recall what it was like to watch the sunrise over Notre Dame cathedral and the Arc de Triomphe, the year I turned forty in Paris.

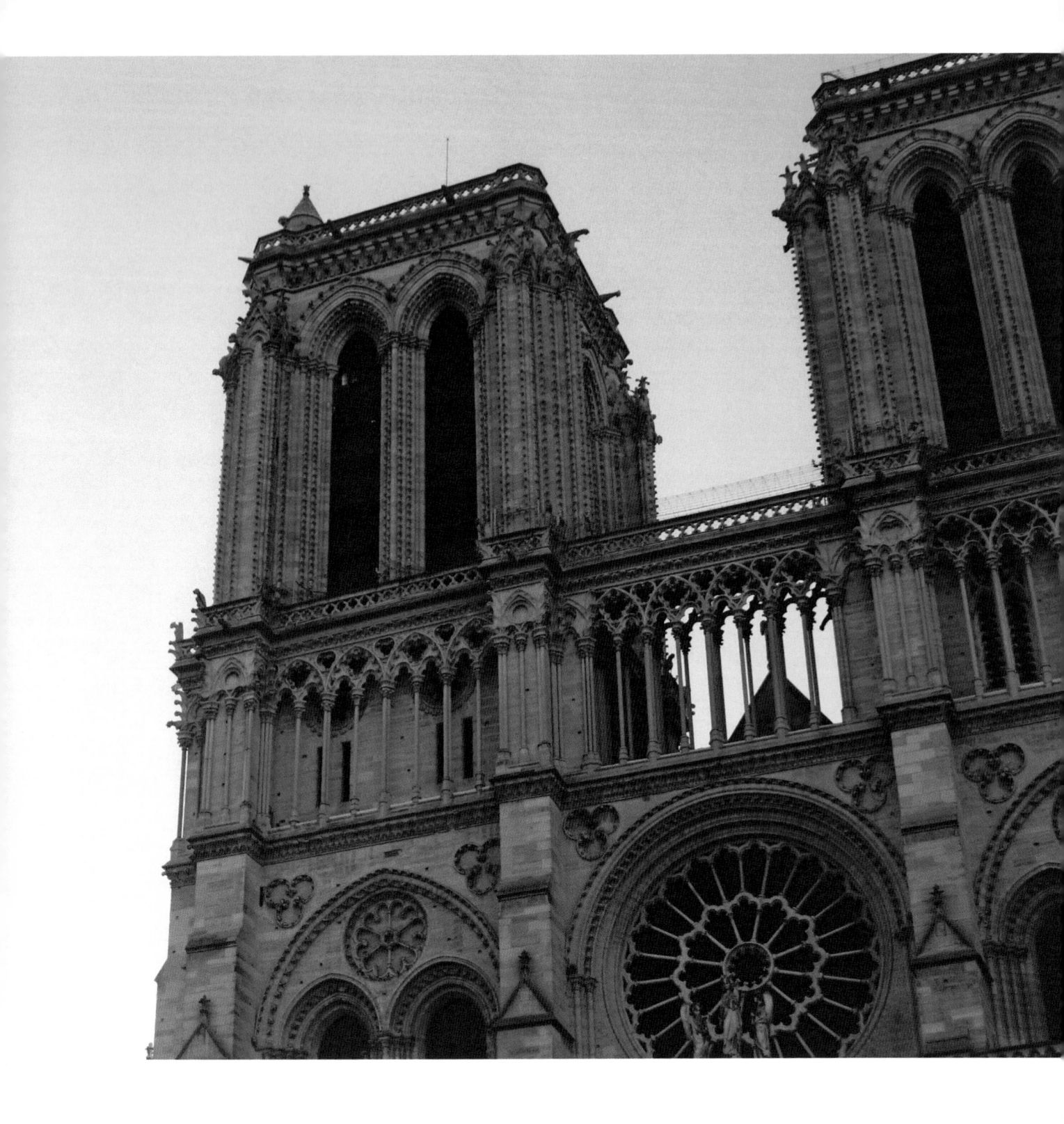

Arc de Triomphe } Day 20 – May 10

In Paris, rush hour begins about 9 a.m. The Parisians work until 7 p.m. They have dinner between 8 and 10, and therefore, they go in later the next morning. Tourists tend to follow the same plan. That is my good fortune. I was so disappointed with the visit to the Arc de Triomphe and the Champs Élysées last week that I wanted to return at a time with fewer people. The massive arch sits on an island in a traffic circle and was made to honor those who died in the French Revolution and Napoleonic Wars. Beneath it is the eternal flame of the Unknown Soldier. May 8th in Europe is Victory Day, which celebrates the WWII surrender of Nazi Germany, and Sarkozy and others had laid wreaths around the flame. I wondered if maybe the best way to see it before the wreaths were removed was in the early morning before anyone else was up. I set my alarm, grabbed a free bike, and made my way across town. The bike ride itself was quiet and pleasant, which on Paris streets is nearly unheard of. I saw one or two lonely café owners cleaning their sidewalks, sadly a few homeless, and a couple of police officers (always good to see when you're a solo female). Arriving at the arch just about sunrise (6:30ish), I found something wonderful. *No one.* It was just me on the island with the arch. I could take my time with photos, really study the art and the architecture, and just breathe. A lovely morning breeze lifted and furled the massive French flag that hangs beneath the arch, and it quietly revealed the place of honor it is intended to be. So it was, as the sun came up, that I captured the Arc de Triomphe, and in my quiet solitude I could let the weight of it capture me.

{ *...in my quiet solitude...* }

De l'eau } Day 21 - May 11

Those who know me, knew it was only a matter of time before this topic came up. If you don't like potty-humor then skip to the next entry as I'm going to be very un-French right now. It's time to talk water, toilettes, and other, well… harder topics. First, *de l'eau*. The drinking water in Paris is considered extremely safe, and they serve it in lovely large carafes upon request. I've heard it said, "The tap water here is perfectly fine, and it leaves more euros to spend on wine!" I'm drinking water like crazy—Titanic proportions. One, because it's so good, and two, because I'm walking so much that I'm dehydrated. I know I'm dehydrated because regardless of how long I'm away from the apartment, I've no need of the public toilets. In the first week of wandering the streets, and probably because of all the exercise, I had to use a public restroom only once. Which reminds me, Paris is great at handling its poop. There are small Zamboni-like cleaners that scour the sidewalks and streets outside my apartment every day. They must, because the pigeons are prolific, and no one picks up after their little *chiens*. We're so fussy at home about picking up after our dogs, but here… wherever! "Wherever" also means they go right into hotels, restaurants, stores, cafés—like Dorothée's Jack Russel, Bandit. I've also found the best way to slow down a Parisian is to stop and lavish their little dogs with affection—*petit chien mignon*! Then they have all the time in the world to spend with you. Just watch your step.

Coffee } Day 22 - May 12

To me, coffee is the drink for adults. I remember being about fifteen when my mother asked what I wanted to drink with breakfast and I said, "Coffee," as confidently as I had seen her do in restaurants. She complied, skeptically, and I tried it. It was undoubtedly the worst thing I had put in my mouth to that point (sorry, Mum), and I wondered why adults raved about needing or wanting coffee. Bitter, acidic… it made me shudder. Many years later, and after many influences from coffee-snob friends and Ted, I've grown somewhat used to it. Now I know how I prefer it, too. I like a strong, dark coffee, with more milk than coffee, and sweetened considerably, and just one cup is enough. That's exactly the way Parisians like it! You can get your tiny little cup of espresso, or a *café noisette* (hazlenut), or other variations. Thankfully, the most common is *café crème*, or *café au lait*. If you think they'll just serve you milk with coffee, think again. The French make an art of something so simple, and each restaurant has its own method. Coffee in a cup with a container of heated foaming milk. Coffee and milk heated and foaming together. *Avec sucre?* Then it comes with paper tubes of sugar, or the lovely cube you can watch dissolve on your spoon. And it's only one cup, no refills, at the end of the meal, which suits me perfectly. Ordering *le café* is a mini adventure in itself for just three or four euros. Which way will they serve it this time? But brace yourself, because it's fully charged rocket fuel. They really should call it café OLAY!

Adventure } Day 23 ~ May 13

As I write this, it's almost 2 a.m. on the 14th, and I've been up since dawn yesterday (13th). My schedule, it seems, is quite askew. Today (yesterday) I woke up at 6 a.m. to go take early morning pictures of Notre Dame before it became Notre Damn Tourists. Then I went to a produce market. A festival for bread-making. A flower market. A bike ride. A half-hour nap. Some writing at home and at a café for several hours (on a novel, not the blog), and then back home to clean up for a Friday night out. I began the night at one café for appetizers, went to another little Italian-owned place for dinner and sat next to a Canadian named Kitty who lives in Hong Kong, then stopped by Dorothée and Bandit's bar for a drink and sat next to an Austrian/American/French guy. Dorothée had me try Get 27 (pronounced Jet 27)—a 27 percent alcohol *digestif* that's supposed to help settle the stomach after eating. Oh, I feel settled all right. And it's not just the alcohol. This is exactly the kind of day I love. In Paris, or even at home. I've been up for 20+ hours, met people from all over the world, had drinks with people (and a dog) who feel like friends after just two weeks, and wandered home feeling fed, happy, a little tipsy, and safe. Tomorrow I might be up at 10 a.m. instead of six, but depending on where I go and when, it will be an entirely different type of day. It's like I'm Alice and I never know which hole the white rabbit will have me take to Wonderland. But shouldn't it be this way, even at home? In the end, isn't life supposed to have been an adventure?

MONTMARTRE

One of the best ways to see some of Paris, especially for those who are not comfortable stumbling around on their own or who are tired of being on their own, is a walking tour.

One day I signed up for a guided, English-speaking tour of the Montmartre district, famous for the Moulin Rouge. There, artist studios abound from historic figures like Van Gogh and Toulouse-Lautrec to current artists selling their canvases in the street.

Our group heard stories as we sauntered down famous and infamous streets of Montmartre. Here, they made the movie *Amélie*. Marcel Aymé wrote *The Walker-Through-Walls,* which inspired the sculpture of a man partially encased in a stone wall. Picasso lost paintings in a tragic fire, and the last surviving windmill still lingers. The tour ended with a glass of wine.

Visit newparistours.com for information.

Bikes } Day 24 ~ May 14

Vélib'. Vélo libre. I have been riding the free bikes all over Paris—what an experience. I can take a bicycle from any rack and return it to any other rack in the city. It's eight euros a week for unlimited rides, and the first thirty minutes are free. There are hundreds of racks, all about three hundred yards apart. The city provides the bikes that each weigh about 20 kilos (40 lbs.). Thankfully, Paris is relatively flat, but sometimes so are the bike tires. My first bike had a seat that lowered while I was riding it. In some areas there are specific bike lanes, but then they'll merge into a lane for buses, taxis, and motorcycles—the three least courteous drivers in Paris. I've biked on boulevards, through (yes, through) traffic circles, and down tiny one-way streets. One particularly narrow street had cars parked on both sides, and my bike lane went toward the oncoming cars. As a car drove toward me, the driver's side mirror was nearly touching the mirrors of the parked cars. There wouldn't be room for me in between if I didn't time things right. I'm certain I had the look of a deer in the headlights when the car came at me on my left. I sucked in my breath and leaned slightly to my right, and I noticed that even the driver was leaning away from me and gritting his teeth. Oh, and this is all without a helmet. Learning the lanes, looking for bike rack locations, and tracking thirty-minutes on my watch, all while peddling in traffic is, well… a little like juggling and trying to ride a bicycle at the same time. I think the liberated part of the *Vélo libre* comes from not only seeing and learning the city better by riding above ground instead of in the metro, but also experiencing the thrill I feel when my thirty minutes are up, and both the bike and I have survived.

TRANSPORTATION

While guidebooks will give specifics about each method, simply trying them helped me discover which mode I loved best. The bike won, but here are a few tips:

~ *Examine bikes. Flat tires and sagging seats are common.*
~ *When in doubt, bike with others through traffic. Plenty of Parisians use the free bikes to get to and from work, so it's easy to find a pack heading your way in rush hour.*
~ *Drivers are just as afraid of hitting a person on a bike.*
~ *I could ride down small streets, or major avenues and see much more of Paris than I could on foot.*
~ *The metro is wonderful when I traveled far, or my feet were tired, but riding underground made me miss Paris.*

Note: A cab is best when it's dark and you're a woman alone. The metro doesn't run all night, and even though the bikes have lights, a taxi after wine is always wise.

Art } Day 25 ~ March 15

Art. Artists. Painters. Sculptors. Photographers. Modern. Classical. Impressionists… How can I possibly sum up art in about forty seconds? Art in Paris is seeing life itself. There is an abundance of it. Much of it is free to see—outside of the busy Louvre and a couple of other museums—and often it's right in the streets, walkways, or gardens. And it absolutely thrills and delights me. It is during the moments when I need a break from the noise and rush of the city that I go in search of it. It is there, in the stillness of a museum or a small tucked-away gallery, that my soul is fed through eyes other than my own. It is among the canvases, sculptures, or objects that I can glimpse what has been, hear a thought unspoken, imagine the possibility of a different life, or grasp an idea that has not yet occurred to me. It is within the brush strokes, a movement, or a defined collection that I can be present in history and see the future simultaneously. With so many voices and so many hands expressing themselves, and all within a city that has been host and home to so many phenomenal artists for hundreds of years, it is impossible not to feel deeply moved. True, I have always loved art in various forms, but here I have found the opportunity to fall in love with it again for new or different reasons. And I am overjoyed.

This woman's expression, in the painting Une soirée au Pré-Catelan *by Henri Gervex, is exactly how I feel when I experience art within the city. The painting is in the free Musée Carnavalet, covering the history of Paris.*

Reflections } TURNING 40 IN THE LOUVRE

The people of the world love the Louvre Museum. Approximately 8.5 million of them saw it in 2009. Open 310 days a year, it is 652,300 square feet of artistic masterpieces on display in the center of Paris. It was a palace before Louis XIV and then... blah, blah, blah. There are more statistics about the Louvre Museum than the 380,000 masterworks it contains. It's downright overwhelming, and with the other 27,419 people that will be joining you per day, it's easy to feel lost before you even get fifty freaking feet from the massive lobby. I was not about to wander aimlessly through that kind of crowd, so the night before I devised a plan.

Turning 40 } ...continued

I reviewed the maps online and wrote out my list to take with me. As soon as the museum opened, I would go the self-serve kiosk to buy a ticket. Pick up a navigation guide/headset. See the Winged Victory statue. Visit the Michelangelo sculpture gallery. Then the Egyptian section. Last, the Decorative Arts wing containing the actual apartments of Napoleon III. I had to leave by 1 or 2 p.m. before I starved to death in some forgotten corner of a Pharaoh exhibit where future visitors would think I was one of the mummified remains.

At 9 a.m., it was all going so well. Tickets and plan in hand, navigation headset hanging around my neck, I went straight to the *Winged Victory of Samothrace*, the sculpture of the Greek goddess Nike. They have her placed on a rock pedestal resembling a large ship prow, at the top of a long flight of stairs, so you approach her from beneath. Art critics have determined her "best side" is a three-quarter view on her left, but I quickly realize, for a woman with no arms or head, she is commanding and stunning from every angle. She is sexy and feminine, yet healthy and robust, with a pair of breasts and an ass that men would die to protect. This sculpture exudes what I imagine most of us women would like to feel like every single day. Brave. Confident. Alluring. Beautiful. Strident. And free. Some believe she is depicted descending from the skies, but placed on the edge of that rock. To me, she seems to be lifting off. She's on the precipice of something even greater than herself. Stepping forward, wings out wide for flight, with the wind of the future already pressing and lifting her skirts.

I wander off envisioning myself feeling that way now that I'm turning forty, and from there, POOF! I was lost in a hallway leading to heaven knows where. Crap. I had no idea where I was. I looked at the map on the 2″×4″ screen of the handheld guide wondering how I could navigate my way back to my plan again.

I took a right into an exhibit room to get my bearings and ended up standing in front of the *Mona Lisa*. She is, I'm sorry to say, not what I expected. I was a little let down that she was so small. The canvas is 21″×30″, and as if to prove the point and make you feel ridiculous for thinking she was larger, the Louvre has placed her in a room with the largest canvas they own—Veronese's *Wedding of Cana* at 391″×267″. As I stood in front of her smirk, I stared into her face and compared her simplicity to the chaos of Cana. I realized the *Mona Lisa* makes a lovely point with her small, demure self. Not overbearing, too complicated, or too grand, it's easy to be with her. Unlike the monster painting behind me, it would be easy to travel with her. Leonardo Da Vinci did. He carted her demure, quiet, canvas visage with him everywhere for more than fifteen years. He began painting her when he was fifty, improving, altering, and working at her continually until right before he died. Hmm. Yes, I'm sure you see the lesson, too. Patience, grasshopper. Building a woman that is both engaging and mysterious takes time, and sometimes you start later in life than you planned. Or perhaps it's like Ted always says, "You don't find yourself, you create yourself." So maybe my strict plan for the day wasn't so necessary.

(far left) An example of the beauty of the exterior of the Louvre looking out from within. (left) The marble statue of Diana of Versailles, *the Greek goddess.*

Turning 40 } …continued

I stuffed it in my pocket and wandered randomly to see what might inspire me randomly. Room after room, hallway after hallway, climbing stairs, and peering at, up, and around masterworks, I learned a few things in those galleries.

Sometimes beauty is on the inside, and sometimes you must look for it outside. With all the artwork on the walls, it's easy to forget to peer through the massive floor-to-ceiling windows and glass doors. The instructions in my handheld guide told me if I was lost to look outside to determine which wing of the giant U-shape I was in. It should tell me to look because it's also one heck of a view. From the top floor galleries of the Louvre, you are finally up over the buildings of Paris and can see the Seine to the south, the city to the north and east, and I.M. Pei's pyramids in the entrance to the west with the Tuilleries further off.

Looking ahead also means keeping a chin up. The ceilings in the Louvre are some of the most exceptional paintings in their collection, guilded with solid-gold cherubs, floral motifs, or marble sculptures. A number of times I stood in rooms with my head back, mouth open in awe. As I turned to go, I would watch numerous people stride through the room looking around or down at their maps and missing the best part.

Sometimes a dead end will lead to a better place. Taking a set of stairs, not knowing where I was, I happily found the entrance to Napoleon III's apartments. I pulled on the door and it didn't budge. "*Fermé,*" a guard sitting nearby said. *Closed.* It turns out the Louvre is so big they have to close some sections each day because there simply aren't enough employees to handle it. Sometimes I don't have the manpower to tackle things that seem overwhelming either. I went back down the stairs only to find signs leading to the Egyptian exhibit. Delighted to be exploring that piece from my must-see list, I wandered through it for a solid hour until I came upon a newer exhibit.

Sometimes digging at your own history exposes the foundations upon which to build. Just thirty years ago, the Louvre excavated its own floors and found the walls of the original Medieval Castle built for Philippe Auguste in the tenth century. Are you kidding me? Until 1980 they had been sitting on an archeological site without realizing it? Now, I'm not going to go home and rip up my floorboards to see what's under my historic house in Richmond, but after seeing what they found down there, I kind of want to. Impressive foundations of the old castle are dug out, and you can walk along the sides of these massive stone blocks still intact that show how the Louvre was originally intended as a castle fortress and an arsenal.

For another hour, I happily wandered past paintings, painters recreating masterpieces, and eventually found

myself in the Michelangelo sculpture gallery, another room from the plan in my pocket. A massive corridor bathed with light, it is filled with the most amazing women. In fact, the Louvre is so proud of their masterpieces depicting women, they have a tour customized to see just them.

In this room is Canova's white marble representation of *Psyche Revived by Cupid's Kiss*. It captures the moment just before their lips are to touch, and she is reclined, open, and naked, and her anticipation of being swept up by him is palpable. It's a few days before Ted arrives, and I can't look at the statue too long without feeling voyeuristic. In complete contrast, in the center of the room, is a sculpture of Diana, the goddess of chastity. She was known for being able to punish the misdeeds of men and is in the process of pulling an arrow from her quiver on her back. She seems to have such self-preservation. Taut and confident. I have felt the positive aspects of both of these women in my life. Open and yielding, yet self-assured. Never the negative aspects at the same time thankfully. A woman is asking for trouble when she punishes a man and desperately needs him at the same time.

Despite the women in the room, the gallery is actually named after Michelangelo because of its centerpiece of his two unfinished works called *The Slaves*. I've admired Michelangelo for years. When I was twenty-four, it took me six months to read Irving Stone's *Agony and the Ecstasy*

because I kept running to the library to look up all the masterpieces he described. *The Slaves* are unfinished. One is at peace. One struggles. One seems beautiful, the other more coarse and violent. Some say they are incomplete because Michelangelo never could get the figures right so he abandoned the projects. Some believe it's because he wanted them that way, after all, are we ever really finished? As I wondered which was true, I remembered a quote from Michelangelo himself, "Every block of stone has a statue inside of it, and it is the task of the sculptor to discover it." My stomach growled. It was nearly 1 p.m., and I was fairly certain it was a long walk to the entrance. It's so easy when you're touring the museum and staring at masterpieces for four hours to forget that you may have conceivably walked eight or ten miles in the Louvre. It was time to head out.

I turned in my headset, and as I rode the escalators up into the glass pyramids to exit, I thought about Michelangelo's quote and decided that at forty I am both the stone and the sculptor. In many ways, I feel like I'm just beginning so I'm certainly a stone unfinished. I have many years ahead to dabble, alter, or create more of myself, with a plan in my pocket, which I am willing to abandon in order to be inspired. So I'm the sculptor. During this five-week stay, Paris and the Louvre would become my chisel. A new fragment of my figure was exposed.

ART & MUSEUMS

{ ...places of history and creativity... }

Beauty } Day 26 ~ May 16

If it sounds as if nearly every bit of my trip so far as been la vie en rose; trust me, it has not. There have been so many places I have had to leave, including what looked like a nice park, because it reeked of urine. Paris men and dogs can't ever seem to hold their pee. I got yelled at out of nowhere near the Bastille today by a bum who angrily said (in French, and then for me in English), "You don't even look French! The hair. The mouth (I was smiling). The legs. You don't fit in at all!" No shit. As if I thought I blended right in with my red hair and translucent skin. Beggars and homeless people like him are everywhere, and it's often very sad to see. I've also taken the subway in the wrong direction twice. I tried a new flea market on the north side of Paris and came home with bites on my arm. Indeed, they had fleas. Last night, I tried a new restaurant that turned out to be the IHOP of Paris except it served lousy mussels instead of crummy pancakes (note-to-self: if there is a laminated menu with pictures, it is going to be bad). Despite moments like these, the journey, in my opinion, has been, and will be, lovely. It's because I now recognize I make two very important decisions every day. First, I get up and tell myself I will focus my lens and my energy on what is beautiful, moving, inspiring, or intriguing and simply let the other things go by. I also say "yes" more than I say "no," and so I'm constantly trying new things. I think those two habits are both worth taking home.

Speaking } Day 27 ~ May 17

I have noticed the locals speak quite softly. Parisian voices are more moderated, the women especially, and the lilt in the speech is sing-songy instead of monotone. By comparison, I can hear the Americans and Germans before I see them, and the Italians are the ones shouting across the streets and waving their arms. The Parisians. Quiet. Subtle. Even if Parisians are sharing your table, you can't hear the conversation. I find it easy then to linger in cafés to write without feeling like I'm intruding. This weekend, I found a nice quiet café in a very chic section and enjoyed a lovely hour of peaceful, quiet writing. Enter the American newlyweds. Within minutes, they began to fight because she wanted a boob job and he thought that was shallow. Two French couples got up and moved—one of them thankfully, because they had B.O. I thought maybe I'd get a journal entry out of it, so I stuck around to listen. Here's what I learned. One, try not to speak so loudly. Regardless of the topic, it just isn't feminine. Two, if others move away from me, it's a sign that either my underarms or my behavior stinks. Three, never ever look to my partner for approval about my own body image, especially in public. I'm not one to promote plastic surgery, but she was asking him for something she couldn't give herself: permission to be happy with who she was. Four, after someone says "boob job" in a café for the eighth time, my ability to not make a joke about my own A-cups being only half-full falls off dramatically. So, I quietly paid my bill and took my own little boobies back to my apartment to work.

(left) Corner cafés, like this one on Rue Montorgueil, feature quiet conversation.

(below) When I took Bandit's photo, he actually sat up straighter and turned away to show me his profile. I assume he thought this was his best side.

{ ...even the puppies are polite... }

Bandit } Day 28 – May 18

Bandit's crab shack, L'Amuse Gueule, is the place where I most often go to discuss French. Dorothée, who studied in England and worked in New York, is brilliant with both languages, and sometimes she gives me free champagne. Today Dorothée asked, "How are you finding the French? To outsiders we can look very stressed." I wouldn't say stressed, but perhaps a better word for how some of them look is… well… *constipated*. You know that feeling when you haven't gone for a couple days, and so your brow is furrowed, and your mouth is turned down and all you do is think about prunes, so your face kind of looks like prunes. That's what some Parisians look like when they just walk around. Like they need fiber (given all the white bread and cheese, maybe they do). But, as I said to Dorothée (I did not tell her she looked constipated, because she doesn't), I have found the French to be extremely helpful, and it's easy to open them up. Just a slight attempt at French, and they step right in to give me directions, help me with sizes in stores, or explain the menu. The policemen are especially great when I'm lost. With very little effort on my part, a small smile, and a nice "*Bonjour, Madame,*" or "*Merci, Monsieur,*" nearly everyone (save the bum at the Bastille) has been a lovely host or hostess for their city. In fact, when I smile and get one in return, they look relieved I am friendly and I feel like the face laxative they've been waiting for. So, if you visit Paris, fear not. Put in a little effort, be a polite guest, and you, too, will find they are so much friendlier than they first appear.

AU
LAPIN AGILE
CABARET ARTISTIQUE
RUE DES SAULES
AU
LAPIN AGILE
CABARET
et Chansons

Reflections } SPEAKING OF FRENCH

Before my trip to Paris, I studied the language knowing it would make my life easier for the month and, hopefully, help endear me to the Parisians who take it seriously—as we all should. French is a romance language harking back to spoken Latin of the Roman Empire, and it's the official language of all the United Nations agencies and many international organizations. In Europe, it's the third most common language after English and German. While I had some French from my time in Canada, it had been fifteen years since I used it, and typically for Americans with our flat, monotone delivery, pronunciation is the biggest problem.

Speaking of French } ...continued

So I worked with a tutor one-on-one, went to a few French-speaking Meetup groups, watched foreign films, studied DVDs and podcasts, and more. As I mentioned on my first day in Paris, I quickly discovered that my French sucked. Really though, it didn't suck so much as I was just afraid to use it. I was afraid I would say things incorrectly, and instead of asking to buy a hat, chapeau, I'd ask to buy a horse, cheval. My biggest hurdle upon arrival was I simply wasn't brave enough to try it. I was afraid they would know I was a foreigner, roll their eyes, and say, "*Merde*, another American comes to Paris."

So I would slowly grope around for words, or quietly whisper, or give up entirely and just simply point and grunt at things. Finally it occurred to me. *You don't know these people. Dive in! If you screw it up, you'll learn. Maybe they'll help out and correct you, or you'll end up with a nice horse. Just start with Bonjour, Madame or Monsieur, and get going.* I'm now convinced that speaking a new language is 25 percent knowledge, 50 percent experience, and 25 percent having the balls to open your mouth and speak it.

As far as the 50 percent experience portion goes, there were two specific methods that helped my French improve more quickly. One was the media, and two was the people (which is where you must find the 25 percent ball factor).

First, the media, namely television, the internet, and advertising. Newscasters, like in the States*, tend to speak with fewer dialect inflections and with no specific accent. So as they constantly repeated each day's headlines, I could stay in touch with the world and practice along with them a little. The printed media—ads all over Paris, and especially in the subways—help you see basic, common French phrases in action. However, the internet, well... that was a surprise.

How many times each day do you look up something on Google? Me, too. A lot. So imagine my surprise to find that Google.com is Google.fr. That's right. All French. Of course it is. Duh? If you search for something on Google, all of the found responses are in French. All of the Wikipedia results. All of the maps and directions. All of the downloading info.

---

* Except Barbara Walters, which is New York/Boston oh-ma-gawd with an actual speech impediment that makes it difficult to pronounce the sound ɹ—which should help her in Paris, because no one could pronounce my name properly. It always came out Kaheene. Frankly, given the speech impediment discovery, I'm surprised she didn't change her name to Babs Wally.

All of the pop-ups and prompts when there are problems with the internet, too. Even the Google Doodles are for French events, people, and holidays. But it hadn't occurred to me that the whole internet experience would be primarily French until I tried to log in to the blog and all the links were in French. *Connexion* instead of *Log-in*. *Privé* instead of *Account*. It's very easy for us in our English-speaking American world with years of seeing the internet our way to just assume we'll find everything English. It reminds me of a joke. How many Americans does it take to change a lightbulb? One. The American holds the bulb, and the rest of the world revolves around them.

The second, and really the best, way to learn French is simply by engaging with the people. One on one, or in groups, there were always people who were willing to help me with structure, pronunciation, and translations, and sometimes it was in exchange for a little English.

Here are a few favorite exchanges. One was at lunch with a friend, whose French is equivalent to my English. When we were struggling to discuss cheese, and unsuccessfully trying to agree which animal it came from, I finally had to imitate a goat, both in sound and by using my fingers as horns, for us to realize we were discussing the same animal. Another was my afternoon with a woman I had met at the Mad Hatter's Tea Party at Shakespeare and Company. We had agreed to meet for coffee a few days after the tea so I could practice French, and she, English. She took me to see Saint Sulpice Church and the Delacroix paintings, after which I mentioned that it was "good Paris has so many churches, because the cheese, chocolate, and desserts are so sinful."

"What is this word *sinful*?" she asked.

I paused and smiled. "It means the food is so good it must be filled with the devil. It is so good it must be bad. So there are all these churches where you can confess what you have eaten, even if you're not Catholic."

She laughed and said, "Sinful! We do not have this meaning." Of course not. The French find pleasure where we find guilt. But this began a trust-filled, helpful exchange of language quirks and differences that was one of the highlights of my trip.

Speaking of French } ...continued

After Ted arrived, we took a short jaunt to Provence to visit a fellow writer and his family. While in the south of France, we stayed with Andrew, his wife Christiane, and their three children. Two of them knew both English and French, so we had some help from someone who could speak more simply, or, quite frankly, more at our level. The best exchange was between Ted and Emily, Andrew's seven-year-old.

TED
Tell me how to translate this phrase.
Qu'est-ce que c'est? What is it?

EMILY
(smiling and frowning at the same time)
That's what is it.

TED
Yes, what is it? *Qu'est-ce que c'est?*

EMILY
No, that's what it is? What is it?

TED
What is it?

EMILY
Qu'est-ce que c'est.

TED
Yes, what is it? Translate it.

EMILY
It's *qu'est-ce que c'est*!

"Who's on first" skits aside, my favorite exchange was with Bandit-the-dog. Bandit is an adorable Jack Russel, and food is his downfall. He works in Dorothée's restaurant all day, and he still begs for food as if he is on his last leg. When he feels you are near enough to finishing your meal, he'll reach up and place his paws on your legs, and sigh... I was not yet done one night and so I told him, "Sit." He did not. You got it. The dogs speak French. Okay, they don't speak French, but they know it because that's all they hear growing up. It sounds silly to even think otherwise now, but when I translated sit into *asseyez-vous*, he finally did. In actuality, Dorothée told me Bandit is trilingual. It turns out he can ignore commands in French, English, and German. While I now know that all my tutoring and DVD work really did pay off, my French has a long way to go. However, I'm so much braver with it now, so I'll push out a sentence, or a word, right or wrong, and just learn by trying it. By saying it. It may take many years, and many more experiences and time within France to become really comfortable, but I'm willing to suffer through more trips to Paris until I'm fluent. As I've been told, I will know I've mastered the language when I am able to joke in French. In the meantime, this WWII American joke *about* the French is all I have:

American to Frenchman: "Do you speak German?"
Frenchman: "No."
American: "You're welcome!"

{ *...a little French with English...* }

Cheese } Day 29 ~ May 19

Why did I eat all that cheese? I did it because it was there, and it was good, and I simply could not help myself. There are almost 400+ reasons to bring your lactose pills to France. One day it was Bleu d'Auvergne that made me moan as I ate it with a fresh pear. Another day, I tried a soft walnut-encrusted one that I swear was made for dessert. Which, honestly, is when most of the cheese is consumed—it comes after dinner. Just a simple goat cheese, or *fromage de chèvre*, is a creamy and delicious finish to a meal here. Today, however, I ate lightly fried Camembert with a cassis (berry) jam and a salad for lunch. It was amazing, soft, yummy, delicate, and the size of a TV remote control. And right now, I'm paying for it. I get it now. That Camembert cheese loaf is why the French have that serious look on their face. It was so tasty, but I feel like I'm digesting that leather shoe Charlie Chaplin ate in *The Gold Rush*. So was the cheese worth it? Oh yeah. Could I (should I) have split it with eight other people in the café? Absolutely. Will I eat more cheese tomorrow? You betchya. There are 396 to go.

Trust } Day 30 ~ May 20

Yesterday, I did a little shopping and had coffee with a woman I had met at Shakespeare and Company, and we practiced our English and French. I wrote for the rest of the afternoon and had a quiet dinner out. It was my last day on my own in Paris. It's Friday morning and Ted will be here in just a couple of hours. Before I begin looking forward to time with him, I think it's important to reflect on the last three weeks I've spent by myself. There were moments when I was lonely or concerned about speaking French. I have been unsure about trying a new food or worried I might be lost a time or two. I didn't know if I'd be able to figure out the underground in London in just two days, let alone get safely back to Paris. But as I rode the bike across Paris this morning—without my map, and simply knowing where I was going—I realized each time I've passed successfully through all those apprehensive moments, it came down to one thing. I had to let go of my fear. Each time I did let go and embraced the new, the awkward, the uncomfortable, or the scary, a remarkable thing has happened. I have found a part of me that is more certain of myself and more capable, even during those times I failed. It leads to "what else can I try?" because more and more I trust me. I believe I can do this. As my time shifts from me to we for these last ten days, I'll have new parts of me to share with Ted. I will leave my journal to go put on the new dress I've bought just for today and head to Café Sully where Ted and I have agreed to rendezvous after he arrives. My palms are all sweaty. I'm so ready to share this with him.

BLEU D'AUVERGNE

11,30 € AOC

QUEFORT
GABRIEL COULET AOC

BLEU DES CAUSSES

13 90 €

FOURME D'AMBERT

1 kg

12 4 €

*The cheeses in France are in abundance, abundantly fresh,
and never more so than in the markets.*

My Love } Day 31 ~ May 21

Certainly before Ted was here, there were pictures, paintings, and sculptures that made me long for his contact or drove me to eat more cheese and dessert than I needed. Hell, I saw neutered dogs getting more action than me. But not now. *Il est arrivé*. He arrived. He was a little delayed, and after a while even the waitress was looking for him as I waited and wrote in the outdoor café. But then magically, there he was, walking toward me. And how was the rendezvous at Café Sully after over three weeks apart? Like a scene out of some sappy movie. The traffic stopped at the perfect moment, I leapt from my chair to run midway across the street, he lifted me into his arms with my foot in the air. The waitress cheered a little. He came to sit, we had lunch together, walked back to the flat, and then… I won't go into all the details (mostly because my parents are reading this) but let's just say it is lovely. Lovely to be strolling through the parks of Paris with a hand to hold. Or to stop in the street for no other reason than to kiss or be kissed. Last night and today, we wandered, had a picnic at the Eiffel Tower under a tree I had found for us, survived a bike trip, and simply sat in cafés and talked (Kindle? What Kindle?). While I had seen some of the romantic side of Paris before, it is clear it's called the city of love for a reason. It's like when you are thinking about getting a certain type of car and suddenly you see them everywhere! It's a PDA party in this town! Suddenly love is blossoming all over. Most importantly, it is right here. "Why oh why do I love Paris? Because my love is there."

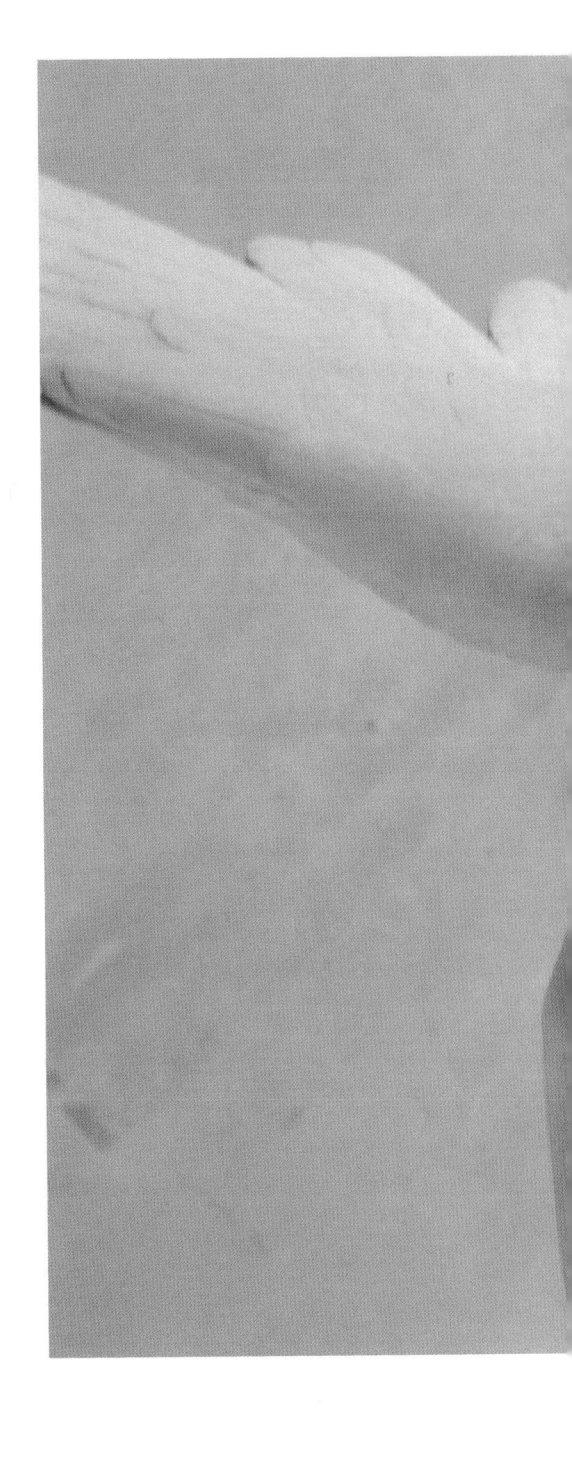

In the Louvre is this statue by Antonio Canova depicting Psyche Revived by Cupid's Kiss, *in the very moment before rapture.*

South } Day 32 ~ May 22

I took 161 photos today. Granted some of them were doubles to get the lighting or framing right, but 161! It's partially because everything is brand new. Monday through Wednesday we are visiting friends who have luckily bought, and are unluckily (because of contractors) remodeling, an old farmhouse in Provence near Avignon. Rather than just take a lightening fast TGV train in 2.5 hours, Ted and I left a day early and rented a car. Our intent was to slow down time and just explore. For a while we were on the main A6 highway, then we escaped onto dinky side roads. Let me explain the views this way: The wish-you-were-here phrase must have been invented on these roads. Old castles literally surrounded by moats. Sheep grazing, alongside stone buildings climbing with roses. Charming towns with blue-shuttered windows. Elegant cathedrals across the street from the main cathedral. Amazing light dappling through trees onto cobbled streets. And us in a little red Fiat zooming down the road alongside old craggy walls that end in little villages containing no lights, but one 1970s shiny telephone booth. The photo opps are remarkable, and Ted was really great about zipping to the curb when I hollered to stop. Although after the second cemetery I had to pull over to see, Ted mentioned, "I read there are 20,000 of these in France, how many are you going to photograph? Just so I know." In some ways, the rolling hills near Dijon, with no fortresses in sight, reminded us both of Virginia, except for all the bloody massacres and an extra 2,000 years of history. So it's a little like home, with a lot of here instead. More adventure waits down the road tomorrow.

Taking what we thought was a wrong turn, Ted and I ended up across the road from Semur-en-Auxois. It was a lovely happenstance, enabling us to pass by the town and the thirteenth-century fortress still standing.

Quiet } Day 33 – May 23

We are, as I would describe, deep in the heart of France. An hour or so east of Avignon, off a road leading to one town, down to another village, and then finally to this small collection of stone homes with terracotta roofs, tucked among rolling hills and cherry trees, with castle ruins on the bluff. It is here with a fellow writer, Andrew, and his wife, Christiane, and their children that I can comprehend the way France breathes and sounds. Is it the steady wind and seasonal heat that cleans the air or the vines that clasp the earth to hold it still long enough so I can listen? I'm not sure. There is the crunch and shuffle of our feet along old stone roads. Sheep bay in the distance, with the whooing of a dove, unseen, nearby. The wings of a praying mantis flitter as it springs onto a shaft of wild grass—the wheat-like grass that sways and whooshes at our feet. When we sit for drinks, or dinner, the climbing roses deaden the roadside sounds of a single car half a mile away, so that the chink of our glasses is only drowned out by the wine gulping for air as it licks and blubs into the crystal glasses. Winston, the family dog, tick-tick-ticks his Whippet nails around our feet, while the children's laughter rings like a wind chime of fat little bells. As the setting sun pulls away the crackle of heat, it is replaced with the singing crickets, and the creaking of wood and hinges on the last of the closing doors. The house settles for the night, and my keys on the laptop seem to be too loud—out of place. It is here, in this quiet place, far away from the city, I feel like I can finally hear.

{ ...I feel like I can finally hear... }

Words } Day 34 ~ May 24

It was our second sunrise in Provence. Today Andrew and Christiane took a holiday from their lives and we just explored the Luberon region—an interconnection of little villages with lavender fields, Roman roads, olive orchards, or goat farms in between. The people, the culture, and the structures are steeped in such immense history. A simple stone bridge still stands that was built in the first century. It is impossible to imagine how many hands built it, touched it, or have given or taken life by crossing over it. The area writhes with a sunlight and feeling that is beyond words. And yet, over many streets and glasses of wine, the conversation often turns to writing, which Andrew and I are both ardently pursuing. We don't just discuss what we are writing—those conversations come easily, and our supportive partners are relieved to hear our behaviors and thoughts are consistent. The more difficult, equally delightful chats are about *how* we are writing—*how* do we fit it in while life goes on around us? *How* do we stay engaged in this life and find moments (or ask for them) to live temporarily in the historical or fictional worlds we are researching or inventing? For these conversations, the words spill forth like the inexplicable brilliant and soothing light that falls at the end of each day in this valley onto its ancient rolling fields. But in this short visit, among the stories we have shared and in the smells, sounds, and sights of the Luberon, we found history. Built friendships. And most definitely uncovered the inspiration to keep going back to the words. So as we close out our last evening here, I'm reminded of this quote by Saint Augustine: "The world is a book, and those who do not travel, read only a page."

This Roman bridge structure still stands and was in full operation up until just five years ago. It was built in the first century! If it still stands, it was done well. That's a good lesson for writing, too.

Reflections } WRITING IN PROVENCE

Have you ever had a beautiful, delicious dream that becomes hazy and fades upon waking, and yet the feeling of it lingers over you and affects your entire consciousness as you make your way through the real world? *That* is Provence.

Painters fall into new sunset colors in their palettes here. Poets write about the vibrating air and the scent of it. Photographers attempt to record the history lurking in doorways and shadows. Artisans try to bottle the essence. It wasn't until I was standing in it myself that I realized none of them got it quite right. They were close to capturing it, but it was hazy, like that dream... Elusive.

Writing in Provence } ...continued

I have reread my entries for those days we toured in Provence. I've reviewed all my photographs of the region (over 450 of them). Still, the sense of the place that lingers from that four-day excursion is more colorful, smells more sweet, tastes better, and sounds richer than I was able to express through either my lens or my pen. I couldn't get it quite right either. So rather than trying to do that again, I have to instead focus on the impressions that linger in me from that brief visit.

We were in Provence not only to see the area, but also to visit with a fellow writer who had recently moved there to the Luberon Valley. Andrew and I first met about three years ago at a San Francisco Writers' Conference. Like the three hundred other attendees, we had the same dream. Give up our day jobs to write for a living. Since then, we have both made lifestyle adjustments, and we are so much closer to living the dream of being paid to write. Our time with Andrew, his wife, and their three children became a glorious few days in Provence, sharing the craft of writing.

My take-away from our lovely chats in the south of France is actually *Fuhgeddaboudit*. How on earth is it that what I remember most is a Jersey term? It started with another funny conversation between Ted (Italian, from New Jersey) and Andrew's three-year-old, Catherine.

TED

Now when you're asked to do something, and it's just not that important, or you're being given something and you don't want it, you say *Fuhgeddaboudit*.

CATHERINE

Forget about it?

TED

No, like this. *Fuhgeddaboudit*. And nod your head using your chin while you say it.

CATHERINE
(perfectly mimicking Ted)
Fuhgeddaboudit.
(Wanders off saying it to herself repeatedly)

While the exchange is obviously funny, within the word there really is a fabulous lesson, especially for writers like Andrew and me. We need to learn to *Fuhgeddaboudit*.

Days in late May in Provence seem to happen in slow motion. The lingering sunrises and sunsets, the pace of the cars, the steep angles of the footpaths and roads, the shimmering heat waves that nestle in the valleys. All those combine to make the day slow down a little. Andrew tells me that if he can just write for two hours each day, the writing builds on

itself at a pace slower indeed, but a consistent one. It helps things grow, like those lazy Provence days. In turn, I share that sometimes picking up the pen, instead of the laptop, helps to slow my thinking. So I can let go of correcting typos and make sure the words are right. *Fuhgeddaboudit.*

As we climbed high to the top of the Simiane-la-Rotonde historic castle and ruins, we talk of how important it is to have an understanding companion or spouse. Writing is a big gamble, especially fiction, and it means a life of uncertainty, of constant revisions, and often of humility. To get the stories right, you need to escape occasionally back in time or into made-up worlds. Like those solid, eleventh-century stones beneath us in the rotunda of the castle, it's so much easier if you have someone to say, "I will lay down solid foundations here on earth so you can walk in the clouds for a while." *Fuhgeddaboudit.*

Lunching on the patio at a café in charming Banon, a lovely red burgundy wine flowed. Ted and Christiane shared their views about the stories we are writing. They laughed at our behaviors and their own. Reading our work, they said, was sometimes torture. "They get one chapter finished," says Christiane, " then share it with us, but there is no more, and we are left hanging." It's like being thirsty and sampling a taste of wine, then not being able to drink the whole bottle for days, weeks, or sometimes months. I see they, too, are gambling on us. They truly believe we will produce a case of award-winning vintage from just one vine. Their belief in what we are writing encourages us, so there is less worry. *Fuhgeddaboudit.*

Creative playtime at the beginning and end of each day is what we received from their children. Having lived without a television and with engaging parents has made the children into these affectionate, curious, and engaging little beings. Eating with us on the outdoor patio as days softly began and ended, they were doodling, involved in discussions, asking questions, and being delightful. They reminded me how important imaginative playtime is. Let the writing go at the end of the day. Pick up a hammer and rebuild a Provence farmhouse. Take photographs. Take a hike. Dig in the garden. Do something other than write. It was like being hoisted up high on a swing with them each day and being given a lovely, soaring shove so I could *Fuhgeddaboudit.*

That push is exactly what writers need. Sometimes that comes from playtime. Or from visiting a fellow writer and his family. It's why writers like Stephen King wrote the book *On Writing: A Memoir of the Craft.* I think it's as much to clarify the process for himself as it is to share his experience with other writers. How many engineers, doctors, therapists, politicians, and others have written books about their work?

Writing in Provence } ...continued

Thousands. But for writers to write about writing? It sounds odd. The only explanation I have is that by jotting down the process—how we write, why we write, how to keep writing—only then can we actually *Fuhgeddaboudit* and get back to the act of writing.

Will I be able to make all these revisions? *Fuhgeddaboudit.* Will I be able to make an income? *Fuhgeddaboudit.* Is the character in the book I'm reading stronger than the one I'm writing? *Fuhgeddaboudit.* Will I get published? *Fuhgeddaboudit.* Will the book sell? *Fuhgeddaboudit.* Just write.

Since returning home, I have been writing more than I ever did before I left, and I'm certain Andrew will be making time for it as well. Without a doubt, his family won't forget our visit. Not long after we left, Ted received a note from Provence. Catherine was up past her bedtime, and Andrew asked if perhaps it wasn't time for her to go to bed. That cute, little three-year-old simply looked up at him, tossed her head from her chin, and said in her best New Jersey accent, "*Fuhgeddaboudit.*"

Wine, nuts, freshly picked cherries, and cheese. The perfect meal to remind me to slow down. Enjoy the moment. Talk about writing. And Fuhgeddaboudit.

{ ...Air. Oh the quiet, quaint air...}

Home } Day 35 ~ May 25

After being away a month tomorrow, I still find I'm craving a little routine or familiarity. I like getting up early in the morning on trips. The light for photography is good, and something about having breakfast each day helps ground me. Early mornings are incredibly difficult when the culture is on a night-time cycle like it is in France. The French ease into a leisurely round of predinner drinks about 7 to 8 p.m. most nights and gradually work through dinner between 9 and 11 p.m. By the time the cleanup is done, and I've readied for bed, it's after midnight. Then the next day arrives with a beautiful sunrise all too soon after only five or six hours of sleep. I've been up late and gotten up early repeatedly, and even more so since Ted has arrived. Add into things our little bit of travel across country, and my body is saying, "Hold on. Can you find something that feels like home, Karen, and go there?" Having just driven back to our Paris apartment from our lovely trip south, I'm surprised to find that feeling of comfort here. In just the four weeks I've been here, this apartment feels like home. There's no doubt the pillow beckoning from the next room is mine now. So while I feel like I've been burning the candle at both ends packing as much as I can into each day (this is not a complaint, mind you—I comprehend my bonne chance with this trip), I'm off to sheets that smell familiar, with a partner that is like home himself, and the hopes of some long, deep shut-eye before Paris picks up again in the morning. No alarms here tonight. I'll let the street sweepers wake us up.

Cooking } Day 36 ~ May 26

Eating out in Paris is delightful. Leisurely meals and unique food options cooked by someone else, while watching people. Eating at home has its attractions, too. Leisurely meals and unique food options cooked by your own hands, even while wearing pajamas. Tonight, we skipped the pajamas, dressed up, went out, and took a cooking class. While it was a bit hurried—two hours, including eating the food, very un-French—we came away with three recipes we didn't know already, plus a few great tips. Do you know when you make a meal for a dinner party you should prepare the food in the reverse order in which you will serve it? Dessert first, prep/prepare the entrée, get yourself ready, and then make the appetizer. The hottest, most complicated things are done first, so you're not over the stove when people arrive. The thing I appreciated most about this particular class was the presentation, and I don't just mean of the finished food. The ingredients were arranged to look as if they were waiting in their best attire to be taken out and dined. I think we can sometimes blow past the preparation process, when really it's the art of making the food that extends the experience.

(left) A light drizzle of olive oil falls onto the fish. It is stacked with tomato, basil, and lemon to be baked in parchment sealed with egg whites.

(below) Our cutting stations in the kitchen.

Once again, despite the fact the course was rushed, it's here that I'm learning to slow it down already! *Don't* rush it. *Don't* shovel it in. Instead, fall into the act of touching, smelling, and truly seeing the food as it combines to create a delicious meal I can savor. This is why the French eat less— simply because they take more time to enjoy the aesthetics of the individual elements that make up the whole meal. Even if it's made at home while wearing PJs, it can still be *bon appétit*!

{ ...the art of making food...}

Jazz } Day 37 ~ May 27

Jazz happened. At night, especially with a loved one, Paris can eat up time in the most pleasant of ways, and tonight I'll blame it on the jazz. So I'm writing early tomorrow (28th), not just late today. Ted has wanted to see a live performance in a Paris jazz club for a long, long time. "So many amazing musicians have started, stayed, or played in Paris," he said. He used to listen to the likes of Miles Davis, John Coltrane, and Robert Johnson in live jazz performances from Paris on NPR late at night, mesmerized. So tonight we ventured via three metro lines into Montmarte—a district known for seedy women, starving artists and writers, and, yes, jazz. What better place to hear it than in a wine cave. We found this tiny gem (all the great Paris places are tiny) on rue Lepic called Autour de Midi... et Minuit—a classic French restaurant upstairs with a *cave voûtée* below. With the David Sauzay Quartet, we found ourselves rhythmically grooving (as much as a Canadian white girl and a man from Jersey can) to the incredible, smooth, and intense quartet + one. Sax and trumpet, guitar, stand-up bass, and a percussionist extraordinaire made Sinatra's "Sunday in New York" seem like an easy Paris walk in the park. In that intimate and ancient-looking cave, the sweet sax echoed off the stone walls to reach the ears of the two dozen or so of us hunkered down in the darkened cellar... and Ted crossed one of his dreams off his bucket list.

Aside from being a lovely place for family outings, the Parc Des Buttes Chaumont, tucked inside Paris, is a common spot to take wedding photographs.

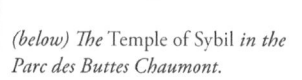

(left) The cemetery is the "retirement home" to the likes of Oscar Wilde, Jim Morrison, Edith Piaf, Chopin, and hundreds more. A map of the top-visited graves is available at the gate for those dying to know where to go.

(below) The Temple of Sybil in the Parc des Buttes Chaumont.

Outdoors } Day 38 ~ May 28

"Saturday, in the park, you'd think it was the fourth of July." As the band Chicago sang, on *le week-end*, the Parisians head out of doors—especially on a 70°, sunny day like today. In front of the massive Luxembourg Palace, you can sit on chairs (not on grass, as I discovered when I was asked to remove myself from it). The Tuileries in front of the Louvre seem to stretch on forever in one dusty, statuesque expanse. You can spot a tourist who has been there by the whitened cuffs on their pants. There are quaint, intimate gardens nestled all over the city. Today, we chose two spots to explore. The first, was Père Lachaise Cemetery.

{ ...let time stand still... }

While we knew it would be quiet because of the inhabitants, it exceeded our expectations as a restful, park-like place. With incredible sculptures, architecture, trees, and stray cats, it is peaceful, despite the eeriness of trees jutting up through ancient graves, and the number of Poe-like ravens cawing as they swoop through it. From there, we made our way to the Parc des Buttes Chaumont, on the advice of Dorothée and Bandit. It was not over-selling it to say it's the most beautiful park in Paris. Waterfalls, a grotto, concrete path railings carved to look like tree branches, temples, and grass you can lie on. There is something sweeter to a park surrounded by big city that heightens my appreciation of them. The sound changes from traffic to breezes in trees. Maybe it's the contrast in color, from city gray to park green. But also, it feels wonderful to let time stand still while the hub-bub goes on outside. It's like the world spins around you while you take in a picnic, a nap, or perhaps a kiss or two. Or three. Or four.

Versailles } Day 39 ~ May 29

I'm not ignoring the fact this is entry 39, or that we must go home soon. Rather, like eating dessert after a long, satisfying and delicious meal, I find the knowledge it will end soon is making me appreciate each moment more. It's as if each of my senses is heightened. Markets have been one my favorite experiences this month, and in the 300+ stalls of the Versailles market southwest of town this morning, the cantaloupe tasted sweeter. The fish was fresher. The flowers' perfume was infinitely headier. The calls of the market vendors sounded more like the music being sung outside this café where we now sit, back in Paris, in the late afternoon. As I write, Ted reads, and we both allow ourselves to be distracted by the people-watching-feast walking by. Or by a pair of blue suede shoes on a man. Or by a Muppet-like dog. Or by the click-click-click of a cyclist on a leisurely Sunday-in-the-city ride. The sky above us is among the bluest I've seen yet, in a month of near perfect weather with only two days of rain—one of which was in London, of course. With three or four more hours of daylight on this next-to-last day, I really must stop writing and go. Not because we have somewhere to be necessarily, but because I have more city to savor with someone I want to hold onto. Or is it someone to savor and a city to still hold onto? Either way, Paris and my love are saying, "Let's go out and explore."

The Versailles market is a haven of tents, tables and pavilions surrounding a traffic- and pedestrian-filled instersection.

Reflections } LIGHT AND LOVE

The two most difficult things to describe about Paris are light and love. Both are in such great, glorious abundance that no Paris story is complete without them. However, in trying to describe them you come out sounding either factual and devoid of feeling, or like fiction, personalized and wrought with feeling.

Factually, Paris has adopted the nickname "The City of Light." It was in part due to Paris being the center of activity during the age of enlightenment. Host to two exhibitions at the turn of the century, Paris was flooded with artists, scientists, architects, and philosophers showcasing new inventions, new designs, a new way of thinking, and new ways of capturing the world.

Light and Love } ...continued

It was for the World's Fair of 1900 the Grand Palais exhibition hall (now an art museum) was built. A massive steel and glass-domed structure placed with a view of the Eiffel Tower along the Seine, it is the largest "transparent" structure in the world. It has the remarkable effect of both allowing light to fill the interior to the point of bursting, while providing an airiness to the solid stone buildings around it that takes the breath away.

The city also acquired the nickname because it was one of the first cities to install city-wide exterior and street lighting. The finest example of which is the bridge built for the same 1900 World's Fair. The Pont Alexandre III bridge is a runway of lights leading to the Grand Palais building. Elaborate, decadent, gold-guilded, cherub-hugged torches line the expansive arched bridge, reflecting brilliant sunshine during the day and illuminating the bridge and waters below at night like white icing on a rich dark-chocolate cake. It's one of a multitude of bridges, boulevards, fountains, structures, and sculptures that is simply aglow after the sun goes down. The whole city is speckled with frosting.

As far as love goes, the fact is, we expect it to happen in Paris. French is the language of love, and Paris has a reputation for it. She has been making out and sleeping around for centuries, so we believe she'll be up for it before we step off the plane—either with our partners or in search of one.

As Ted, a psychotherapist, says, "We are so conditioned, so primed for love that we are open to it. We expect to experience it there. So we do."

We do so because of one heck of a marketing campaign. In addition to "The City of Light," Paris has adopted the nickname "The City of Lovers." It's in the artwork like Canova's *Psyche Revived by Cupid's Kiss* in the Louvre. It's in the music. Ella Fitzgerald, Louis Armstrong, and Frank Sinatra all sung about love in "I love Paris." It's in the movies—*Midnight in Paris*, *Forget Paris*, *French Kiss*, *Last Tango in Paris*, and *Moulin Rouge*. It's in the museums and in literature. There are even books about the best places to kiss in Paris, with "at the Rodin Museum in front of The Kiss," always making the list. Because it is everywhere, and has been well documented, we are conditioned. Primed. Programmed. Ready. Doomed. Doomed to being a hopeless (or really, hopeful) romantic wandering the streets of Paris with a love-struck look on your face.

But those are just the facts. That's not how it *feels*. There were two moments in Paris where I truly *felt* light and love combine to the best effect. I sigh even now, just thinking about them. They make me all warm and squooshy. They are both so clear to me that it's as if they happened just today.

The first was while we were bicycling along the Seine near the Grand Palais, our tires crunching through the gravel. The mid-afternoon sun was dappling through the thick canvas of leaves overhead, falling randomly onto the dusty path ahead of us. Ted and I rode on opposite sides of a long row of Chestnut trees, seeing each other in between the darkened trunks, like a movie-reel slowed so you could see every photo-perfect frame.

Racing ahead, or slowing down, we played hide-and-seek between the trees. We took turns taking pictures of one another. We marveled at the views of the bridges, the Seine, and the Eiffel Tower. Our laughter wrapped around trunks ahead of us, fell behind us, or was carried away on the wind. In light. Out of light. Into the shade. Out of the dark. Coming together at the end of the long, long row of trees, onto the same path. Into full, warm sunshine. One hand on the bike, our other hands reached out to hold onto each other. Our souls fell more in love with each ray of light that warmed our faces. Paris. In love. In broad daylight. We were "twitterpated," as Thumper said in *Bambi*.

A few days before we left, we experienced Paris's light at night. The evening was so magical, that even now bits of it are clear and parts of it have faded like fog. I don't remember if my hair was up or down. So, I'll say it was down, and the curls bounced across my black silk blouse as we walked across Île St.-Louis. My light gray lace and toule skirt swished as I walked in my high heels across the cobblestones. The metal lock and key I had asked Ted to bring from home jangled in my silk handbag next to the few euros I had dropped in earlier. Ted's brown, Italian shoes clicked in time with mine as we walked west down the Rue Saint-Louis toward Notre Dame. With his shirt-sleeves rolled up, a scarf wound round his neck, and his dark, flat-front trousers, he looked more European here than I remember seeing him at home. I grabbed his hand in mine and leaned into him to wrap my other around his wrist as we walked in step together. The last remnants of blue and white light were being stretched out along the buildings and brick streets ahead of us. Their facades glistened as if wet from rain.

"Where are we headed?" Ted asked. As we reached the end of the island and crossed over to another bridge, I explained. "We are going to the Pont des Artes bridge, also now called the Lovers Lock Bridge. It's a newer tradition here, whereby lovers come together. You attached your lock to the bridge, throw the key in the Seine, and so your love is bound forever." He stopped walking, met my gaze, squeezed my hand, and sighed.

We simply could not have timed it better, even though the timing was completely unplanned. From the bridge, we could watch the setting sun duck behind the buildings,

Light and Love } ...continued

setting them alight with oranges, yellows, and reds, as if all of Paris were burning with passion. The fading day made the waters of the Seine run like molten silver below us. Together we hooked on the bronze lock, made to look like gold in that warm light, and closed it with a small click. We grasped the key in between our touching palms. We waited as a white boat sailed by and giggled at the thought of our key landing in a passenger's lap and going with them back to Pasadena.

As the boat slipped under the bridge from view, and with one last long, lingering kiss, we threw the key into the water together. We watched it make a slow, swirling flip, like in slow motion, as it reflected the last rays of sun and slipped into the Seine with a small plink. I imagined it falling into the silt and foliage below, sinking into the darkness,

rotating and slowing turning to sand to erase any possibility of unlocking our love.

Awww maaaan! That even sounds like fiction! It's hard to believe it happened that way, but I swear it did. I could have said, "We put it on the bridge along with the other billion locks they have to cut off every few months to make way for more, then we threw the key in Seine as the sun set, and now somehow our love will last forever." But telling it that way would have been a lie. In the least it would not have been the whole truth of the matter. What does matter is that this was my experience. *That* is the way I saw light and love in Paris. It's impossible to explain it because it's not that way for everyone.

Would it have been different for Hemmingway? For Edith Piaf? For Toulouse-Latrec? I'm certain it was. Would it have been different for Ted? I have no doubt, and he was right there with me.

But these moments were mine. I absolutely know, without a doubt, that love and light are both simply there in Paris, in all their glorious abundance, for the taking. So while I was there I was hopelessly in love. Hopefully in love. Happily lit up. Wonderfully doomed. Luckily, it all came home with me, too.

"My happiness is to be near you. Incessantly I live over in my memory your caresses, your tears, your affectionate solicitude. The charms of the incomparable Josephine kindle continually a burning and a glowing flame in my heart."

~ Napoleon to Josephine in a 1796 letter.

Parting } Day 40 ~ May 30

It's after midnight here in Paris, and we've exhausted the day. Beginning at 7 a.m. we packed in a drink or two at cafés, Napoleon's tomb, and the armory; biked to Notre Dame; walked hand-in-hand, dined at home with pesto-stuffed gnocchi from the Versailles market; and more. Yet if I add today to all the others, the number of events, places, sights, and experiences I have not seen in the city far, far exceeds those I have. Paris simply offers so much. When I came during a brief five-day visit fifteen years ago, I sampled the city and liked it instantly. But much like relationships, both parties must be ready to fully engage for love to blossom. Perhaps Paris was ready then. I was not. I needed more life to happen first. I needed jobs, a career, a few moves, some losses, and most certainly a healthy relationship to be able to do a trip like this. Experience has allowed my pen and lens to grow sharper so I could truly see the city, her people, the sights, the smells, and the sounds, and comprehend the effect on me. *Here, food is art. Art is in small details. Details are found when you slow down to smell the flowers. Flowers make people happy. People add more to life than anything you can buy.* Every event and moment has delighted me each day in part because I was simply open and ready for the experience, and as a result I'll be taking home with me not only a deeper liking for Paris, but now a love for her as well. A French way to say "I love you" is "*Je t'aime.*" The beauty of the phrase is in the verb, "*aimer,*" which means "to like." So for the French, to love someone is to truly like them, and if you truly like them, then it is natural to love them. I understand this implicitly now. They go together. And now, sadly, we must go together, home. We have just one more moment to hold onto each other in Paris, and the plane leaves tomorrow… *Au revoir Paris. Je t'aime.*

We kissed at sunset, took a final nighttime bike ride along the Seine, held hands, and fell more in love with Paris and each other over one last drink. Yet, there is still so much to do. I guess we will have to return.

Epilogue } June 3

It's hard to let go, isn't it? It feels odd to be back in Virginia knowing the Paris I walked in each day still goes on without me. Dorothée still serves up drinks and fresh crab each day, and Bandit still begs as if I never fed him. The man on the corner still puts out his fresh produce and waves. I envision it like a time-lapse film. Bikes are coming and going from the racks, traffic and pedestrians still dancing around each other, and cafés are emptying and refilling as nights fall and days begin. *Sans moi.* Reacquainting myself here is equally odd after a month away. I sat quietly in my home-office and marveled at the layer of dust that had settled on the books, desk, and shelves in my absence. Five weeks in my day-timer are empty as if I did not exist during that time. I am forgetting to check the cell phone after being so disconnected from it for so long. *Disconnected* is exactly the feeling I have. I went off and lived a completely different life for five weeks, and even though I'm glad to be here with Ted and our cats in our own home, now there is a new part of me here that wasn't before, too. It's the part that lived a dream. Has seen, tasted, touched, smelled, and felt extraordinary things. Made some new friends. Fell in love with a city, and with Ted, even more. I'm glad this new bit of Karen is with me now. Now, I'll always have Paris.

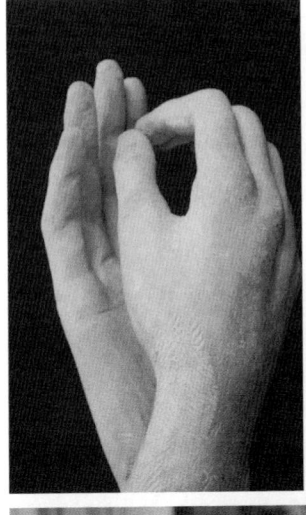

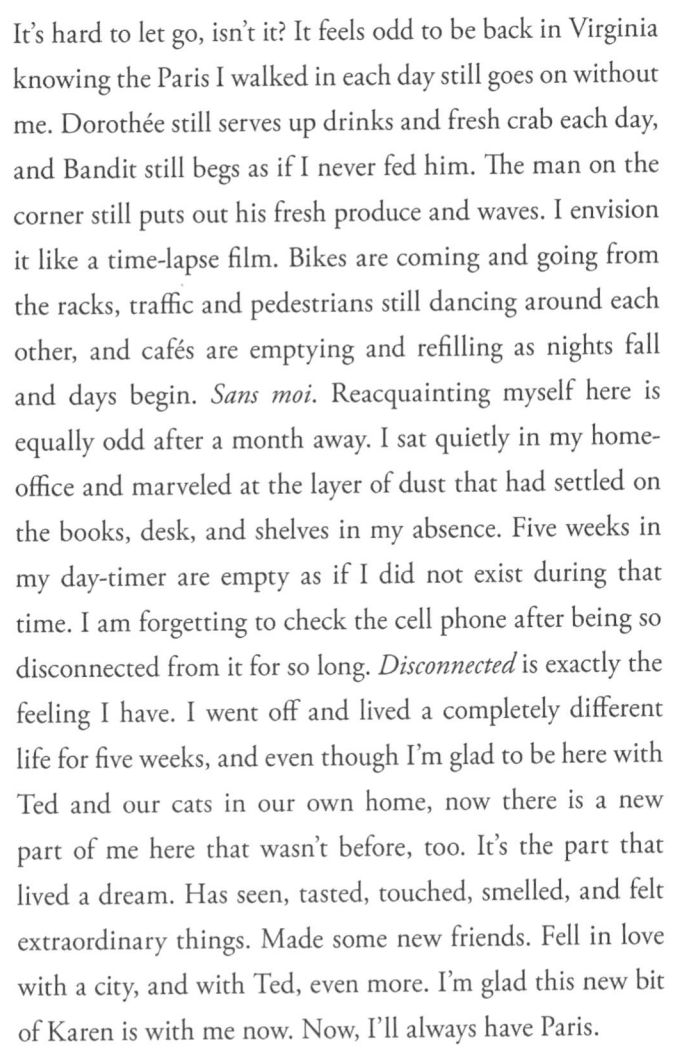

In the end...

Since my return home, I'm once again reminded that memory changes over time. Reading my entries only a month or two later, they feel like slow-motion movie footage of Gene Kelly dancing along the Seine—graceful yet from so long ago. Already, my memories are sepia-toned and the glitter flakes off and sticks to my fingers each time I take them out. I've re-read every entry, written my reflections, and reviewed the pictures and maps. I've laughed reliving moments with Ted, and I've shared stories with friends who begged for details. It is all an attempt to seal the edges of the best memories before they fade.

At night, I dream about Paris. I am speaking French and even little Bandit nods and understands my longing. I daydream about walking along Boulevard Morland, tasting a fresh baguette in the morning, kissing under the Eiffel Tower, or riding the bicycle to the Arch de Triomphe with the wind in my hair as the sun rises over the city.

I hope my brief visit enabled the people or places of Paris, even in some small way, to be touched by me. Perhaps Dorothée tells of the Canadian who stayed for a month while Bandit barks as he chases my shadow down the street.

{ ...I dream about Paris... }

Or there is a new, unspoiled pillow in the apartment. Or maybe, somehow, my laugh has been rolled into the breeze blowing off the Seine and new visitors are infected by it, too. How I hope the new parts of me I pulled, chiseled, and enjoyably discovered in Paris will stay with me like a favorite song. Playing over and over again. Although my memories of Paris will surely soften with each day, I will always carry with me this feeling. "I lived in Paris once, when I turned forty. I was so incredibly happy there."

So, alas, I must close and return to my life here. It's impossible to end a journal about a voyage to Paris better than Hemingway did in *A Moveable Feast*.

There is never any ending to Paris and the memory of each person who has lived in it differs from that of any other. We always returned to it no matter who we were nor how it was changed nor with what difficulties nor what ease it could be reached. It was always worth it and we received a return for whatever we brought to it.

When, oh when, shall I return? Soon, I hope. Hmmm... perhaps I should go somewhere new instead. Yes, perhaps. But where?